COLCHESTER

An Early Walk

A Humorous Look at People of Colchester's Past

Compiled by

John M. Hedges

Illustrated by

Stan Amey

&

Andrew Dodds

Foreword By

Patrick Denney

Colchester Historian

Published in 1997 by John M. Hedges
6 Ash Road, Alresford
Colchester, Essex CO7 8DU

hardback ISBN 0 9530633 0 5

British Library/Cataloguing in Publication Data.
A catalogue record for this book is available from the British Library.

Reprographics by LazerType, Colchester

Printed and bound by
The Bath Press, Bath

Front cover shows Major John Bale's picture of Colchester High Street, and the Old Town Hall about 1890.
Completion of the water tower (Jumbo) in background 1882, and the present town-hall 1902.
Photograph supplied, courtesy Colchester Museum Resources Centre.
Back cover picture from Essex Ballads, There's olluz summat by Andrew Dodds.

CONTENTS

This book is dedicated to my grand-children, Mark and Stephanie,
also to the memory of my dear Father

INTRODUCTION

Four years ago, a company that I had devoted 30 years of my life to decided in their wisdom to thank me very much for the service that I had given them, due to the changing scene, the streamlining of the industry, it was now time to depart.

This, I thought was an excellent opportunity to do the many things that had not been easy previously. Walking in the Lake District, travelling more widely, painting, cycling and photography, these were things that my wife and I thought we could both enjoy to the full

How wrong could one be!

Some six months following my retirement from work and immediately after the Christmas festivities, I was struck down with a brain haemorrhage which resulted in quite a long spell at the Colchester General Hospital, my physician commented afterwards, I believe I complained about some minor irritation, "you are a very lucky man" "you should be in the crematorium".

Well, that's all in the past, I had to get on with my life.

Born 1931, in a very old Tudor style building, opposite the Old Rectory on East Hill in Colchester, I moved into a newly erected council property at Old Heath on the outskirts of the town. Here I lived through the second World War experiencing with thousands of other children the Traumas of air raid shelter's, gas-masks, soldiers frequently on the move, search-lights and barrage-balloons in the skies, bombs dropping, rationing, and eventually evacuation to another part of the country, in my case, it was Burton Latimer in Northamptonshire.

Much more recently, I discovered from a relative that between the years 1863 to 1905 when he died, my great grandfather was a Custodian of the Colchester Castle, a Police Constable in the Borough Police Force and a Turnkey (gaoler) for the borough Gaol.

My renewed interest in Colchester's past had begun, but I must confess, with not too much enthusiasm until one day, some friends told me that they had some old newspaper cuttings that I might be interested in.

Some time later, when they paid me another visit, they were laden with two well known supermarket bags loaded with what I can only describe as old dilapidated and crumpled newspapers, collected over the years by their parents. After sifting through each and every single column and page, I realised what a veritable treasure trove of Colchester's past history I had in front of me, one which I was unable to ignore, so here I am today 1996, writing and collating some of these amusing and humorous stories which include Gossip from 1823, to ballads and poems, from the early part of this century.

I hope that whoever reads this book will obtain as much pleasure from it as I have had in writing and bringing it all together.

John Hedges
Local historian

FOREWORD

Those of us who have an interest and affection for the historic town of Colchester and its extensive hinterland will again rejoice at another literary excursion into its past.

This present volume is the result of many hours of sifting and sorting through local archives to bring together into one collection a veritable storehouse of local anecdote, humour and prose. Poems by local authors including the famed 'Essex Ballads' by Charles Benham, and humerous snippets of life as seen by our indigenous forebears all serve to illustrate the richness and diversity of our native wit and humour.

Focussing mainly on the 19th and early 20th centuries, the book is divided into three main chapters each concentrating on a differing aspect of anecdotal humour and literary wit, whilst combining with the help of numerous illustrations to achieve an agreeable blend of amusement and anticipation.

What, for example, was it like to take a stroll through Colchester in the 1820s? What kind of humour made our forebears laugh? What kind of words and phraseology did they use in their everyday speech? Now is the time to turn the pages and find out.

I recommend this book to you and I hope you enjoy reading it.

Patrick Denney
Colchester Historian

ACKNOWLEDGEMENTS

I wish to acknowledge my grateful thanks to the following people who have helped me to make this publication possible.

I would like especially to express my gratitude to William (Bill) and Anne Long of Colchester, who have provided me with so much information. My sincere thanks also to David Clark for his unstinting interest and assistance; Stan Amey of Clacton on Sea for his illustrative contributions; Andrew Dodds for allowing me to use the original illustrations contained within the 'Essex Ballads' publication; Anne and Ray Milburn, 'Essex Ballads'; Patrick Denney, Colchester historian, for his interest combined with the foreword to this book; Andrew Phillips, Colchester historian; Hervey Benham Trust; 'Essex County Standard'; Local Studies section at the Colchester Central Library; Martin Winter, Colchester Museum Resources Centre; Ken and Rita Sharpe of Thorrington; Ruth Davies, Alresford Pointer; Alec Corton for his unstinting help and patience with various computer problems that I have encountered; Ronald Lucas and Arthur Payne for their help concerning Amian Lister alias Nicholas Olde, Alf Wakeling, curator, Brightlingsea Museum, and Pat and Gordon Green, Wivenhoe.

To those who have contributed items of information, but regretfully whose names may have been overlooked , I offer my sincere apologies.

Sources:

The combined newspaper's of the Essex County Standard; West Suffolk Gazette; and the Eastern Counties Advertiser. The Local Studies Section of the Colchester Central Library.

CONTENTS

Illustrations

Photographs

Poems by Nicholas Olde and Ken Sharpe

Part One

Short Stories 1929/30

The pace of life in the early part of this century was considerably slower than that of today. The everyday family of farmers, land-workers, thatchers, blacksmiths, fishermen and the many various craftsman, all had much time to discuss and exchange stories at the end of a hard days work in the field, or at sea, these exchanges usually took place at their local inn or hostelry.

The combined periodicals of the day, the "Essex County Standard." the "West Suffolk Gazette," and the "Eastern Counties Advertiser" invited their readers from Colchester and its extensive hinterland to submit humorous stories each week in exchange for prizes, the conditions that they imposed for entry were as follows:-

**10/- EACH WEEK FOR BEST EXAMPLES:
5/-; 2/6 SECOND; 2/6 THIRD**

Contributors to the short story competition are asked to confine themselves to actual local incidents and to guarantee that they are stories that have not already been published. Many of the stories received are disqualified as being old and familiar chestnuts camouflaged as local stories. Competitors will please note that such Contributions are not desired.

The stories at that time were quite humorous and now give one an idea of life in those bygone days. I have made a few random selections from some of those stories and included a few illustrations which I hope will amuse and bring back a few nostalgic memories for many.

A Large Order

During a Nature Study lesson in Standard II. At our Council School last week, the common nettle was taken for the subject. The teacher having taken the lesson, the schoolmaster asked several questions, and mentioned that some people made Nettle tea, when a little boy promptly said "Please sir you can get 'Nettles' milk."
Burnham on-Crouch.

MISUNDERSTOOD-I was watching the cricket match between Essex and Notts. last Wednesday and sat near a gentleman in plus-fours who, apparently, had brought his wife to see her first game. When A. Staples appealed and Hipkin was given out by the umpire after scoring only 4, the following reached my ears:-Wife: "Is he out, dear? "Hubby: "Yes, lbw."-Wife:"Hush, Harry! I thought it was only at golf that you swore!!"
Wivenhoe.

TWISTED-Some boys were playing marbles and falling out over it in the Castle Park. "Call yourself straight" said one. Why if you put a handful of nails in your pocket they'd come out screws."
Colchester.

TERSE!-An overseer in charge of a country section of the railway in the neighbourhood of Colchester, had been reprimanded for sending in lengthy reports. "All I want you to do," said the superintendent, is to report the condition of the track as you find it, and don't put in a lot of needless words. I want a business report, not a novel." A few days later a section of the railway line was badly flooded. The overseer wrote his report, which ran as follows: "Sir-Where the railway was, the river is."
Blackheath.

WHEN GENEROSITY FAILED-A newly engaged young man living in Colchester, informed the lady of his choice, aged 24, that he was sending her on her birthday, a bouquet of roses-one for each year of her age. He called at a florist's shop, telling the proprietor to send the lady two dozen of the finest roses he could procure. "He's a good customer," remarked the florist to his assistant. "Put him in an extra half-dozen". Strange to relate the florist lost his customer, and, the engagement was broken off.
Wivenhoe.

MAGNIFY-Staying at her grandma's for a holiday last year, little Mary, having been in the garden playing, suddenly felt hungry, so, running in to grandma, she asked for a piece of cake. Grandma, who was reading at the time, put her paper down and went to the cupboard and cut Mary a piece. Mary, looking at the cake solemnly, said to grandma, "Granny, do your glasses magnify?" "Yes dear," says granny. "I thought so," said Mary, "by the size of my piece."
Colchester.

TAKING NO CHANCES-My little nephew, aged six, was, on returning from school, told always to wash his hands, because, as his mother told him, little boys never know what they have been touching. One day the child came home, went straight to the scullery and began washing his face! His father, noticing him, drew his mother's attention, saying, "Look at that boy washing his face." Imagine their surprise when the boy answered, quite seriously, "Well, dad, you never know what I've been looking at!"
Birch, Colchester.

A LARGE ORDER-A very large and portly lady entered a draper's shop in Colchester, and said, "I would like to see a jumper, my size, please." The new young girl assistant to whom this remark was addressed, recovered sufficiently from her amusement to say, "And so should I ma'm."
Wivenhoe.

"I would like to see a jumper in my size."
"And so would I ma'am."

OUR ENLIGHTENED AGE-December 8 being my birthday, I asked my grandson, aged 4, what he was going to give me. His reply was, "Nothing." "What will you give me when I am old and walk with a stick?" I asked him. "I'll take the stick away from you and hit you with it," was the curt reply.
Wivenhoe.

THE DIFFERENCE-An old gentleman from Surrey and very proud of it, walked into a butcher's shop in Colchester on Saturday morning and said "I want a sheep's head please." The butcher said to his assistant "A sheep's head for this gentleman, John," As the boy passed out of the door to fetch it the old gentleman called out, "and mind its a Surrey sheep's head." The butcher who did not approve of his customer's tone called out "Take the brains out, John."
Great Bromley.

TIT-FOR-TAT-A Brightlingsea youth went to a Colchester tailor to have a summer suit made. Whilst having the first fitting last Friday he told the tailor that he was afraid he would not be able to pay for the suit until the end of the month. "Oh, that will be quite all right, Sir," the shopkeeper assured him. "Thanks, very much!" said the youth, "when will it be ready?" was the reply.
Wivenhoe.

THE WRONG SPIRIT-The carol singers were singing outside MacTosh's house when the collector asked him if he would help the carol singers. "I'm very sorry; I have lost ma voice, but I will hold the light if ye like."
Dedham.

1st prize.

QUITE-"Confound you sir" roared the officer to the Army Clerk. "You've addressed this to the Intelligent Officer, you ought to know there is no such person in the Army. Re-address it The Intelligence Officer."
Colchester.

2nd prize.

LOT'S LOT-A public auction had been advertised, and a local farm labourer decided to go along to see the fine old furniture which would doubtless be offered for sale. After looking round with a friend, and critically inspecting the bargains, he paused at last, gazing in awe and mystification and murmuring to himself, "Lot 14, Lot 15, Lot 16, etc, "By gum, that fella' Lot hasn't half bought some stuff; he must live in a darned big house!"
Colchester.

3rd prize.

A BROAD HINT-One day while I was waiting at the North Station, a well known lady was travelling back home with her usual baggage, golf clubs, etc, when she said to the porter, "Have I got all my luggage in the carriage, and are you sure I havn't left nothing behind, "Nothing, ma'am, "not even a copper." the porter replied.
Alresford.

Sizing her up

TRADE UNIONISM-Some men were recently taking the road up at Colchester, and one of them had his pick above his shoulder ready to strike a blow when a nearby whistle went. "Leave yer pick up in the air, Bill," said his mate, "it's one o'clock."
Shepherd's Bush.

IN THE DAYS OF THE THEATRE ROYAL-Doubtless many readers may remember the visit of the late Mr.J.L.Toole to the old Theatre Royal, Colchester. The great comedian played to a bumper house, and at the fall of the curtain there were shouts for "Speech, speech." Then Mr.Toole appeared, and, facing the vast audience, said in a harsh, hoarse, voice, "Ladies and gentleman, I pray you will excuse my speaking, etc. I have received such a 'Cold-chester' I cannot speak. Words are altogether out of the question."
Dedham.

CARRIAGE NOT PAID-Carry your bag, sir? asked a boy of a man hurrying to catch a train at North Station. "No," was the reply, "Carry it all the way for twopence," said the boy. "I dont want it carried," snapped the man. "Don't you?" asked the boy. "Then what are you carrying it for, mister?"
Elmstead.

EXPOSED-Our teacher was doing her best to explain the points of the compass to her class. "Willie Jones," she said, "step out here for a moment." Willie did as he was bid. "Turn round and face the North," ordered the teacher. Willie turned round and faced it. "Now, what is on your right hand?" A flush crept over Willie's face. "Please,Miss," its toffee. I hadn't time to wash it off before the bell went.
Aldham.

T FOR TWO-George was a new hand employed on a local farm. His first job was to stand some bags of turnips and potatoes in the corner of a barn and to mark them so that they could be picked out without any bother. Later the farmer returned to find he had put the letter T on all of the bags, and asked him why he had done so. "Waal," replied George, "I've put T on some for turnips, and T on t'others for taters."
Stanway.

HORRIFIED-A little girl of six years was very interested in watching her auntie make some custards, but when she began to grate some nutmeg over them,"Oh, auntie," the child exclaimed," My mummie often makes custards, but she never puts dirt on the top."
Brightlingsea.

WRONG NUMBER-A policeman had received complaints about a certain hedge being damaged by boys, and one afternoon he came along and caught a small lad scrambling through the same hedge. Catching him by the collar, he demanded his name and address. "What's you're number? "he said. The little chap, looking very scared, blurted out "7728." "Don't be so ridiculous," said the policeman, "there isn't such a number." "There is," said the little boy," it's on my mother's back door," It was her share number at the stores!
Lexden.

TWICE AS MARVELLOUS-An argument occurred between two men about an airman landing safely from a tremendous height, on only one wheel. One of them argued, and got quite excited about it. "He was the only one who had been known to do so," he said. His pal, on the other hand, said "Why, it has been known for them to land without any wheels." "Well, how? "he answered. "By parachute," was the reply.
Elmstead.

SIZING HER UP-While waiting to be served in a shoe shop, I was rather amused at the following conversation. The assistant approached a customer asking, "What size shoe do you wear madam?" "Well," replied the customer, with a charming smile, "I bought size four last time." The girl assistant looked puzzled. "Yes, madam, I remember,"she replied," but you're buying this pair for yourself, aren't you ?"
Ardleigh

THE ONLY DRAWBACK-An army officer asked a body of recruits if they had any complaints to make, and one stepped forward and declared he had been supplied with a ginger-ale bottle that contained, not ginger-ale, but benzene, and that he had unwittingly drunk half the benzene "All right," replied the officer; "You had better not smoke for a few days.
Layer-de-la-Haye, near Colchester.

"What shoe size do you wear, Madam?"
"Well, I bought size four, last week."
"Yes Madam, I remember, – but you're buying this pair for yourself, aren't you.?"

A SHOP-KEEPER'S INDUCEMENT-A notice was put up in a village shop window a few miles from Colchester. It read "Given free with each quarter of sweets." Everybody was curious to see what was given free. One customer, after buying her quarter of sweets, looked into them and exclaimed "What's given free, Mrs.Jones? I can't see any thing ?" "The paper bag, of course," was the reply.
Blackheath.

WHAT A DANGEROUS PRACTICE!-A nervous old lady was travelling from Ardleigh to Colchester by bus recently and was sitting next to the driver. She was very much alarmed, because the driver kept putting his hand out to show the direction he was going to turn. At last the old lady could stand it no longer. "You just keep your hands inside" she said, "I will tell you when it rains."
Ardleigh.

EDUCATION-Two patients, one a farm labourer and one a road mender, had beds side by side at the Hospital, (No. 6 Ward). The road mender was very fond of jeering at the labourer for his country brogue; in fact the road mender thought his position in life far above his neighbour's. This amusing incident occurred during the mid-day meal. The farm labourer called "Nurse. Are there any more spuds? " Nurse. "Any more what? "Road Mender. "He's ignorant, nurse. He means taters."
Colchester.

AWKWARD-A family kept a parrot. These birds being very delicate and susceptible of cold, this Polly was located, temporarily, during the very severe cold of the winter 1928-1929, in the warmer region of the kitchen. There, as is the nature of parrots, it picked up undesirable fragments of talk. When the weather became warm again, the parrot returned to its old quarters in the dining room. The first day of its return, when the lady of the house rang the bell for the servant to come and clear away, came the voice of the parrot "Let 'em ring again!"
Dresden.

PROVIDENCE'S ERROR-Some years ago I knew a farmer at Wigborough who complained bitterly to the minister of that parish of the terribly bad weather for his crops. The minister reminded him that he had much to be grateful for all the same, and "Remember," said the minister, "Providence cares for all; even the birds of the air are fed each day." "Yes," replied the old farmer, "off my corn."
Blackheath.

TWO LIARS-A soldier in the army went to his officer and asked leave to go home and help his wife with the spring-cleaning. "I don't like to refuse you," said the Officer, "but as a matter of fact I've just had a letter from your wife, saying that you are no help to her with the spring-cleaning, and asking me not to give you leave." The man saluted and turned to go. At the door he stopped, turned, and remarked: "Sir, there are two whopping liars in this Regiment, and I'm one of them. I'm not married."
Colchester.

OBEYING INSTRUCTIONS TOO LITERALLY-The shop manager impressed upon Simpkins the need for resourcefulness and tact when-ever a customer made any complaint. As an example, a lady who complained of the inferior quality of some silk which she had purchased was courteously assured that the trouble would never occur again and was entirely due to a temporary disease among silkworms. The following day Simpkins was attending to another customer, who complained of the inferior quality of some tape. Remembering his instructions, he said, "We are extremely sorry, madam, but I assure you the trouble will never occur again; it was entirely due to a temporary disease among ____" At that moment a pile of goods fell on the floor with a deafening crash. The ever resourceful manager had overturned them just in time.
Brightlingsea.

EVIDENTLY CENSORED-A local farmer attending Colchester market one Saturday, was passing a church in the High Street, when he was thus accosted by a priest standing outside the church, "Won't you walk inside? Service for men only." The farmer in consternation exclaimed "What? Is it so bad? If it is not fit for the women to hear, I am sure it isn't fit for anybody."
Brightlingsea

Didn't expect much

EKEING IT OUT-One day during the late war, when rations were threatened, a feeble minded old lady in Wivenhoe entered a grocer's shop to purchase some tea. "You can't have only a quarter, ma'am," the grocer said; "we have to use economy with tea now you know," "Oh, well, give me a quarter, then, and a quarter of what yer just said just now; I expect it's no use grumbling.
Alresford.

WHY HE LIVED?-An old sailor was entertaining a lady visitor at Mersea. "You mean to tell me, "said the lady," that you are the only survivor of six shipwrecked sailors, and that all you ate for a week was your boots? How is it that you are alive while all the rest are dead?" "Well, you see mum," he replied. "I took a larger size in boots."
Colchester.

THOSE LITTLE THINGS-Two friends had celebrated the previous evening and were discussing the matter in the more sober frame of mind usual after an event. One was inclined to be philosophical over the matter, and after giving air to several platitudes and his friend's discomfort, remarked, "You know John, it is always the little things in life that cause us the most trouble." "Ah!" remarked his friend dolefully" that's very true, last night I found my house all right, but I couldn't find the keyhole!
Colchester.

"BOTH HOGS-A motorist was driving from Mersea at a very moderate pace. He arrived at Abberton without mishap, and very steadily rounded the bend. Suddenly another car rushed round the corner in the opposite direction. The steady driver found himself precipitated into the hedge, whilst the other came to grief in the road. "Road-Hog," angrily called out the man from the bank "Hedge-hog!" cheerfully responded the other.
Colchester.

NAME, PLEASE-A high-powered sports car dashed through a small village on its way to Colchester. The village policeman, observing its approach, majestically planted himself in the middle of the road with his arm upraised. With a grinding of brakes the car came to a standstill a few feet in front of the constable. "Come on, what's yer name?" he growled. "Vivian Demetrius Fortescue," replied the driver pompously. "None o' that now," answered the representative of law and order; "I want's yer name-not yer family motto!"
Colchester.

IT PAYS TO TELL THE TRUTH (Sometimes)-Little John, aged seven, stole into the drawing room, and found his mother resting on the couch. Sidling up to her, he said in his best company manner "Oh, mummy, you do look tired!" Mother regarded John wearily, "Yes, Johnnie, I am tired. So very tired that I can't move a hand." "Oh!" responded John, in evident relief, "then I want to tell you I've eaten some of the strawberry jam."
P.G. Colchester.

ANOTHER ORDER-It was evening and the proprietor of the little confectionery shop in Brightlingsea was panting as he struggled with the shutters of his shop. With a sigh of satisfaction he had just fixed the last board, when a small girl touched his arm and said "Please will you take all your shutters down again? I want to see what I can spend my halfpenny on.
Colchester.

WHEN FALSE SEEMED TRUE-A country squire had only one natural leg, yet so well did he use a false limb that even the local country folk were unaware of the fact. The squire, who was an enthusiastic follower of the hunt had the misfortune one day to break the wooden leg. One can well imagine the astonishment of a new servant when the groom burst into the kitchen and said "Master has had a fall and has broken his leg and I have to hurry back with another one." The kindly explanation of an older servant relieved the anxiety of the newcomer.
Blackheath.

DIDN'T EXPECT MUCH-Overheard on the quay at Wivenhoe last Sunday morning:- "Hulloh, Joe! Lovely weather isn't it? "Yes, not so bad for a small place like this!"
Wivenhoe.

"Hallo, Joe!"
"Lovely weather isn't it?"
"Yes not so bad for a small place like this!"

SWEET INNOCENCE-Picking up the evening paper last Saturday I expressed my sorrow that the Essex cricketer chosen to represent England has scored a "Duck" in the first innings. A lady friend, looking at the scores a few minutes afterwards, said; "How nasty of them to print his name O-Connor !"
Wivenhoe.

CROWN HIM-A schoolmaster once asked his class if any boy could ask him a riddle he could not answer, he would give the boy a crown (5 shillings.) He started at the top of the class and went on till he got to the last boy. "Now, my boy, can you give me one?" "Yes, sir," replied the boy: "Why am I like the Prince of Wales?" The schoolmaster replied "I am sure I don't know. The boy replied. "Because I am waiting for the crown," and he got it.
Ardleigh.

INDEED A MIGHTY MAN- "Oh, mummy," said a little boy who had just returned from a walk round Elmstead, "I've seen a man who makes horses; real live ones." "But are you sure, dear?" asked his mother, somewhat puzzled. "Yes," replied the child. "He had a horse nearly finished when I saw him. He was just nailing on its back feet."
Wivenhoe.

Knew by experience

MODERN WIRELESS-A lady in Colchester had just employed a new maid. After the maid had swept the parlour, her mistress went to inspect it. "Haven't you seen this" she asked sternly, pointing to a cobweb across the ceiling. "Yes, mum," was the cheerful reply; "something ter do with yer wireless, ain't it?"
Colchester.

JEALOUSY-Two labourers were discussing the dismissal of one of them from a local engineering works, "Well," said the aggrieved one, "you know that the foreman's job is ter stand about and watch us at work?" "Yes," replied his friend, "but what's that got ter do with it?" "Why, he got jealous o'me, for some o' the other chaps thought I was foreman," was the reply.
Blackheath.

RUNNING WILD-A little boy from London was staying in Colchester last week, and while walking down High Street he said to his cousin, "What's on today? What do all these flags mean?" "Why," replied the other, "our Oyster Feast is to-day. You look out for the Mayor; he'll have a collar and chain on," "Will he?" said the little Londoner; "our's doesn't; they let him run about free."
Blackheath.

BROTHER IN THE WAY-Mary Jane was visiting her aunt one day when a neighbour called. She inquired of the aunt how old her niece was. "You are nearly five, aren't you, Mary Jane?" "Oh, no, auntie; I can't be five until my brother gets off of it."
Boxted Hall.

MORE THAN WAS WANTED-The wife of a Colonel whose regiment was stationed at Colchester once sent the following note to one of the captains; "Colonel and Mrs. Robinson request the pleasure of Captain Jones and company to dinner on the 30th." She received a severe shock when she read the captain's reply, which was as follows; "With the exception of three men on leave and two men sick, Captain Jones's company have very great pleasure in accepting your kind invitation."
Colchester.

MAKING SURE-An old farmer and his wife boarded a motor-coach at Colchester to journey to London. The farmer seemed quite concerned about his wife's comfort. "Are ye all right, Mary?" he asked as they sped along. "Yes, Garge, quite," she replied. "Be they cushions nice and comfortable?" "Couldn't be nicer," purred his wife. "Yer not being jolted?" "No Garge, not in the least." "Don't feel any draught?" "Oh no, none at all," "Well, Mary, yer change places wi' me then," said the attentive husband.
Colchester.

COMMON SENSE-A youth employed in a local office slipped out to a Colchester barber's shop to get his hair cut. But he had not been there long when, to his dismay, in walked his employer, also for a hair cut, who, on seeing his employee, exclaimed "What's this, Jones; having your hair cut in office hours?" "Well, sir, it grows in office hours, doesn't it?" The employer paid for two hair-cuts!
Colchester.

KNEW BY EXPERIENCE-A Wivenhoe gentleman asked his neighbour if he knew the best way to make grass grow on a bare patch. "Yes," replied the neighbour, "plant either vegetables or flowers !"

A DIFFICULTY-A man came up to a house in Kelvedon the other day and asked for a meal. The lady in the house asked him if he could take up the potatoes. "Well," said he, "I can, but don't you think the man who planted them is better suited for the job? He knows where they are."
Kelvedon.

TOO TRUE-A soap-box orator was holding forth at Clacton, and in conclusion turned to his audience and said, "Is there anything that creates more poverty than horse-racing?" "Yes," replied a voice from the back, "betting!"
Wivenhoe.

"How do I make grass grow on a bare patch?"

NO CRIME IN THAT-A resident of Alresford, when walking in the orchard, saw a gang of boys just outside the gate, and one small boy crawling through. The man called out sharply, "What's that little boy doing?" The spokesman outside answered in a surly tone, "He aint doin' nothin'-he's only gettin' out."
Alresford.

MORE THAN ENOUGH-A local football match was to take place, and, finding that the referee did not turn up, the captain of the home team turned to a small spectator; "Look here, you know enough about the game to take his place." Small Spectator. "I know enough about the game not to."
Fordham.

POOR BABY-Baby was taken very bad whilst you were out, mum," said the new servant, "but he's better now. He seemed to come over faint, but I found his medicine in the cupboard." "Found his medicine? Good gracious, what have you given the child? There's no medicine in the cupboard." "Oh, yes, there is mum; it's written on it," and the girl triumphantly produced a bottle labelled "Kid Reviver."
Colchester.

HANG THE CONSERVATIVES-A few weeks prior to the last general election a number of farm labourers were busy at work in a field near Colchester. Suddenly a heavy rain came on and a hasty retirement was made to a neighbouring barn. Discussions on politics formed the chief topic of conversation among both young and old. Arguments as to the respective merits of the candidates waxed hot and furious and generally ended where they began. When the storm had passed over and the men were returning to work, two of the older men lagged a little behind. "What did you think of the arguments, Charlie?" said the younger of the two, "Not much," said the elder; but I will say what I always did say, hang the Conservatives. I always did vote blue and I always will vote blue, that's what I say and I always will.
Eight Ash Green, Colchester.

LITTERS-The week-end visitors to a certain village not far from Colchester scattered the fields with rubbish to such an extent that the residents decided to call a meeting. Accordingly, the vicar said to one of the old farmers in the district "I hope you will attend the anti-litter meeting we are holding next week." "No," the old farmer promptly retorted; "I don't approve of these new ideas, I don't want any birth control for my pigs.
Wivenhoe.

ONE BY ONE-A grocer in Colchester had secured the contract to replenish the store of a small steamer lying in the Colne. When his messenger attempted to board the boat to effect delivery he was accosted by the mate, who in surly tones enquired his business. Upon being acquainted with the messengers intentions, the mate replied "All right, you, needn't come aboard; just throw 'em up one at a time." "Ahoy, there; look out!" cried the man, as he threw a small dried pea towards the mate, "I've a hundred-weight of these!"
Colchester.

UNEXPECTED-A certain young man of Wivenhoe called at the house of a lady friend, and while he was seated alone in the room with her became rather restless. By his manner, the girl knew what was coming. "Hilda," he managed to say at last, and continued with a voice that seemed rather hoarse, "would you, could you, do you think you-" "Please go on, Jack," Would you please, er-er could you get me a drink of water? I am so dry," he said.
Wivenhoe.

VOTES FOR CATS-A Labour canvasser calling upon an old fellow was pleased to hear of the arrival of a family of kittens, all Socialists, Calling a fortnight later, he enquired about them. "Would they be interested in politics?" "Indeed, they be all Conservative now." "But why the change?" "Ah," said the old chap, slyly; "they've had their eyes opened since you were here last."
Dedham.

Strange

HE KNEW-An office boy in one of the large offices in the town had been discovered telling untruths. "Do you know, my lad," said a kindly clerk, "what happens to young lads who trifle with the truth?" "Certainly," was the prompt reply, "the boss sends 'em out as travellers when they grow up!"
Bromley.

TOO RISKY-An old lady called on the vicar of an Essex Church and asked him to come and see her daughter, who was lying seriously ill. "Certainly I will come if she is so bad," he said; "but I have never seen you before; you don't attend my church, do you?" "Oh, no," she replied, "we are chapel people and we didn't like to risk our own minister coming. You see, my daughter has scarlet fever."
Colchester.

TIME-A taxi-driver, who had fallen upon bad luck, had obtained a position as bath chair attendant at Clacton. His first engagement was with an old retired Indian service Colonel, all gout and liver. After pushing the Colonel about for some time and having arrived at the foot of a fairly steep hill, the attendant consulted his watch, and ceased pushing the Colonel's chair. That worthy gentleman inquired with some heat the cause of the delay. "Well, guv'nor," said the attendant, "you'll 'ave to get out and walk now. Your hour's up, see!"
Colchester.

A HINT TO HER-A rather inquisitive woman eyed with extreme disapproval an angler landing his catch successfully on Clacton pier. "Oh, poor little fish," she murmured. This remark greatly annoyed the angler, who had been patiently awaiting a bite for several hours. "Well, madam," he replied, "if it had only kept its mouth shut it wouldn't have got into trouble."
Colchester.

CHEAP AT THE PRICE-During a conversation re electric lighting at West Mersea; "we are having ours put in free. Then we shall have to pay eightpence a unit and three pence for the inspiration."
West Mersea.

AN EASIER JOB-A young man living at Copford, who had worked on a farm all his life, thought he would like a change and joined the Army. When he had been there a little time his officer asked him how he liked it. He said "Very well." All the time I worked on a farm my master never told me to stand at ease.
Colchester.

A SWEEPING REPLY-A lady living in Belle Vue Road, Wivenhoe, has a lovely shrub of white bloom in full blossom. Speaking to two friends at her gate and learning that they were on their way to the cemetery in order to tend and tidy up a relatives grave, she asked one of them if she would like a little broom. "No, thank you very much," replied the friend "I've got a little brush in my bag."
Wivenhoe.

WHATS IN A NAME-On Monday I took my small son for a walk along the side of the river at Wivenhoe. Feeling tired I sat down on the bank and watched the sailing boats. "Can't I go for a sail?" he asked. "No!" I replied, "not to-day; you went out with Mr. Sainty only last Thursday!" "Well, can I have a bathe?" was the next question, I told him I was sorry, but I had not brought his bathing costume. "Well, can I just paddle?" he asked in desperation. Again I refused, as I thought it was too muddy. "Well, what are we going to do?" he queried. "Oh, just sit here and watch the boats," I replied. "Oh, now I understand why they call it a bank holiday!" came the surprising answer.
Wivenhoe.

MARKETS AND MATINS-Several years ago a new vicar was established at Elmstead Church who had previously been a prison chaplain. During a drought the crops suffered so badly that the farmers asked the vicar if he would pray for rain. "Well," said he "I can do so, but I don't think we shall get it while the wind lays where it is." However, he prayed for rain, and it did come, on a Sunday. The vicar, scanning his congregation, noticed that most of the farmers were missing. In his address he remarked "The rain has come, but where are the farmers who should have come to offer thanks?" If it had rained cats and dogs on Saturday it would not have prevented them from attending Colchester Market."
Alresford.

STRANGE!-Some years ago a local labourer living in Ardleigh was going to his work in the morning along a by-road, when he met a stranger, who asked "Where do this road go." He replied, "I don't know where it go to of a night, that's allus here when I come of a mornin'."
Colchester.

"Where does this road go?"
"I don't know where it go to of a night."
"Thats allus here when come of a mornin."

NOT FINISHED-"What are you doing!" asked little Betty's mother coming into the nursery. "I'm drawing an elephant," replied Betty as she put down her pen. "But where is its trunk?" asked her mother, "Oh, that's still in the ink-pot!" answered Betty, as she prepared to continue her work.
Wivenhoe.

Group of children in Wivenhoe High Street, 1910.

The Diplomat

EASILY DONE-Two young men who worked on neighbouring farms were interested in a notice on a board at Bromley about a forthcoming dance. "Are yer coming, Jake?" asked one. "Me go ter a dance!" exclaimed Jake; "does yer fink oi could ever dance boy?" "Course yer could, mate," was the reply; "it's easy; all yer got ter do is ter keep turnin' round and wipin' yer feet."
Great Bromley.

WHY WORRY?-On arriving late one night at North Station, a little girl and her mother entered an omnibus bound for home. The little girl was very tired, and her mother was continually telling her not to go to sleep. After a while, wearying of this, the child greatly amused the other passengers by exclaiming, "All right, mummy; don't worry; I shall wake up again."
Colchester.

SO WAS SHE-The church of a certain small village in the locality was presided over by a gentleman distinguished for his learning and the position he held at his University. One day a visitor was talking to one of the parishioners and the conversation turned to the vicar. "Your parson is a very clever man, you know," remarked the visitor; he's a Wrangler. "Dear me," was the reply, "I should never have thought that, though I always knew his missus was."
Colchester.

WASTED EFFORT-Two small boys had been instructed by the school doctor to visit a neighbouring surgery for the purpose of being vaccinated. They approached the doctor's house very timidly, and were obviously nervous of the forthcoming operations. As they entered his door: "Ah," said the doctor, "let me see, it's vaccination for you two, isn't it? left arm, old fellow, please." A look of intense dismay, overspread the lad's faces at this. "I knew it, Jack," said one, turning to his companion; "Just our luck, and we've both been and washed the right 'uns!"
Colchester.

WILL IT BE PUT BACK?-A Wivenhoe lady was trying to explain to her small son that on Sunday next all clocks and watches would have to be put back, as it was the end of summer-time. "Oh, so Daddy will get back the watch the pickpocket took in London last month," was the hopeful reply.
Wivenhoe.

GETTING WEAK-An old man who lived near the Recreation Ground, Colchester, had been on the retired list for a long time. He was in the habit of walking steadily round the recreation ground each morning. "His constitutional," he called it. After he had recovered from a serious illness, however, he found that his strength was some-what impared. "Yes," he said to his wife, as he returned for the first time after his illness, "I used ter walk right round the rec. every morning, but now I feel so tired when I gets'alf way round that I have ter turn round and come back again."
Colchester.

TIT FOR TAT-A bricklayer was applying for a job at Lexden. After the usual questions had been asked, he said to the foreman, "I'd like to work here, but I can't find a place to park my car," to which the foreman replied, "I guess you won't do. This is a high-class job and we only want bricklayers who have chauffeurs."
Colchester.

A PROFITABLE POLICY-At a country inn not far away from Colchester there hangs on the public bar a portrait of Mr.Baldwin. A friend of the inn-keeper, knowing him to be a staunch supporter of Liberalism, was rather surprised to see the picture given such a prominent position."Why do you display a portrait of the recent Premier?" asked the friend; "surely it is not an advantage to the cause you favour?" "Well, you see it's like this," replied the inn-keeper, "most of the people who come in here know my policy and begin arguing about the picture, and wondering whether I have changed my views. Arguing makes them sit here; they get thirsty, and, well, I think that picture is an advantage to me anyway."
Wivenhoe.

A HOUSING PROBLEM-A little boy aged four was walking down Brook Street, Colchester, with his father, and when they came to some newly built houses with a large notice board in front, said: "Daddy, what does that board say?" "Freehold houses for sale," replied the father. The child reflected on the answer for some time, and then said, "But, daddy, there's four new ones!"
Colchester.

A HANGING JOB-A little boy had just returned to Colchester after staying in London with his parents. He was describing some of the sights he had seen to his little friends, and one asked, "Did you see Pentonville, where they hang the murderers?" "No," replied the young traveller, "I dont think so; but I saw the Royal Academy where they hang the artists."
Colchester.

A SENSELESS QUESTION-During a political meeting in an Essex town, a man put his head in at the door of the meeting room and shouted, "Can anyone here sell me sixpenny-worth of sense?" The audience was amused at this remark, but the chairman immediately silenced the intruder by replying, "Yes, but you have nothing to put it in."
Wivenhoe.

SHADY WORK-The jobbing gardener had finished weeding the path and was resting on a hoe. The lady of the house therefore sent word by the servant that he was to repair the pergola by the lawn. One can well imagine the man's surprise when the maid told him that he was "to look to the burglar by the lawn."
Colchester.

A NECESSITY-One very stormy Wednesday evening the congregation who had arrived for the mid-week service in a village church consisted of a minister and John the verger. The minister expressed his disappointment, saying, "Surely, John, if you and I could venture out in the storm there are others who could come ." "Deed, sir," said John, "if you and me wisna paid for it we wouldna be here either."
Elmstead.

AWKWARD-I was dining out the other evening in Colchester with some friends of mine, and sitting opposite to me was an old lady. She seemed very interested listening to the music. When the waiter came along she asked him to find out the title of the piece they were playing. Other duties claimed the waiter for a time, and when he returned the lady had completely forgotten her request. Imagine her confusion when he bent towards her and softly whispered, "What can I do to make you love me?"
Ardleigh.

THE DIPLOMAT-At a local election meeting a candidate was making himself very unpopular with the working men present by attacking all forms of drinking. At last he began to sense the bad feeling he had created, and endeavoured to retrench with as much grace as possible. "Friends," he said, at the beginning of my speech I said I would advocate raising the price of beer to a shilling a pint, but I ommited to tell you that I would also introduce a measure to have pint mugs enlarged to the size of gasometers." (Loud applause.)
Berechurch.

"Wotcha, think of the new size pint 'arry."

"BEAST"-LY-Two lads were discussing the merits of the cuisine in their respective households. "My mother," said one, "gets three pennyworth of bones from the butcher's and when she's finished boiling them they make delicious brawn." "My mother," said his companion," often buys a bullock's or sheep's head and they make lovely pork cheese."

DANGER OF SOCIALISM-A gang of workmen were busily engaged installing a new fuse-box at the corner of Roman Road, Colchester. A tripod consisting of three stout poles was arranged to take the pulley blocks to allow the box to be lowered into position. On top of this tripod was a large red flag to warn approaching traffic. A bus from one of the country districts came to a standstill against this to allow two passengers, an elderly man and his wife, to alight. The man decided to have a closer view, but his wife, being of a cautious nature, and catching sight of the glittering array of brasswork inside the box, clutched his arm, and whispered nervously "Don't yer go over there, Bill; it looks loike one o'they infarnal things, I thinks they calls 'em, what the Reds have been lettin' orf in Berlin."
Colchester.

ROBBED!-An old countryman was walking along the road at Blackheath, Colchester, when he met an acquaintance whom he had not seen for weeks."Hello, Willie," he said, "whoy y'are a looking bad." "Aye," replied his friend," Oi 'ave jest a-bin in that Co'chester 'Ospital and the doctors have tooken owa' ma appendix. "These doctors'll tak' onything. It"s a pity ye didn't have it in yer wife's name," said his friend sympathetically.
Colchester.

LIKE FATHER-"My dear," said a young wife to her husband, on his return home, "the baby has been trying to talk again." "What was he talking about?" enquired the father. "Well, I think it must have been politics." He started very calmly, but in a few minutes he was as red in the face as could be. "Its perfectly wonderful how he takes after you."

FORCE OF HABIT-A young mother carrying her baby entered a butcher's shop. The shop was rather full at the time, so to pass away the time the woman entered into conversation, the baby being the chief topic. Soon a heated argument was in full swing, the point being the weight of the infant. The mother to settle the discussion asked the butcher to weigh the child, to which he obligingly consented. After manipulating the weights in his accustomed manner he called out loudly, "10Ibs. with the bones, mam."
Colchester.

ANIMAL OR BIRD?-Some years ago, whilst out walking in the town with my husband and daughter, who was then a very small child, we saw rather a nice dog. My daughter being very fond of animals, stepped forward to stroke the dog, and as I knew this kind of dog to be rather ferocious, I exclaimed, "Oh! do be careful; it might 'fly '
at you" My daughter looking very mystified, asked, "But where are the wings, Mummy?"
Colchester.

A WRONG MESSAGE-The vicar of a country church asked his clerk to give out the following announcement: "Next Sunday there will be no afternoon service, as the vicar is going to officiate for another parson." Being rather deaf, the clerk gave the message as, "Next Sunday there will be no afternoon service, as the parson is going a-fishing with another parson."

Knotty problem

HAS HE CHANGED?-My father was having tea with us one day last week. During the meal our little son said, "Mummie, sometimes you call Granddad, 'Dad" and sometimes 'Grandad.' Why don't you always call him 'Dad,' because he is your daddy, isn't he? At least he was when you were a little girl."

DISARMAMENT AT HOME-A certain gentleman, well-known for his frequent appearances in court to answer charges against the motoring laws, was accosted in Colchester High Street by another, who said, "Excuse, me sir, but will you give me a penny?" "Certainly, I will, if you will tell me what it is for." "Well, you see, sir, whenever a policeman dies we collect pennies to pay for his burial." "Here's a half-crown, go and bury thirty."

TALE OF THE DROUGHT-Little Mary, of Rowhedge, had been instructed that it was very wrong to waste water during the shortage of this commodity, and was not allowed to fill the bath in order to play with her boats. When on the following day she was told that her father had got water on the knees, she looked horrified and exclaimed, "How wicked of him!"

HER WEEKLY-In a little Essex village there had been a robbery at the mansion, and the local constable had been given charge of the affair. "Madam," he said, proudly to the owner, "can you remember on what night you heard strange noises in the grounds?" I am afraid I can't" replied the lady; "all I know is that I was in my bath at the time". The constable held up his hand. "That is sufficient; I have it, it was on Saturday night."

LITTLE BY LITTLE-A lady wishing to have everything up to date for her new baby entered a shop to buy a pram. She was shown several which did not seem good enough. At last one was shown her at 20 guineas. "Yes," said the lady, "I should very much like that, but it is rather more than I can pay." "Well," said the shopkeeper, "how about installments," This the lady agreed to, and left the shop with the pram. On going to pay the last instalment the shopkeeper asked how the baby was getting on. "Oh, splendid, thank you; he gets married tomorrow."

HIS WISH-After a recent welfare lecture, in Colchester, the lecturer was speaking to a burly navvy. "So you envy Diogenes, do you?" he inquired. "To be sure," answered the navvy. "But you don't mean to say that you envy a man who lived in a tub?" reasoned the speaker. "A Tub! Blimey! I thought you said Pub," he answered.

WHAT AN ASS-I had just left the Clacton Bowling Green when I saw a little girl, accompanied by her parents, looking intently towards the donkeys. "I want a donkey ride; I want a donkey ride, mummy," pleaded the little one. "Be quiet," said her mother. This did not satisfy the child, who continued to ask so persistently that the mother at last said to her husband, "Jack, for goodness sake take her on your back for a time, so that we can have some peace."

IMAGINARY-During a recent visit to a school in Essex, an inspector examined a class in geography. "Now, boys," he said, "can anyone describe to me what the Equator is?" "Please, sir," said one, "it is an imaginary line drawn round the earth." "That is so," said the inspector, but do you really understand. For instance, could you tie a knot in the Equator?" "Yes, sir," was the prompt reply. "Indeed," was the surprised remark, to which the pupil added, "An imaginary knot, sir."

BREAKING IT GENTLY-After an accident in a foundry one of the workmen was sent out to acquaint the victim's wife of the tragedy, "I've come to tell you," he said "that your husband has happened with an accident." "Oh, dear, what's wrong now?" asked the woman, very much alarmed. "He was over-come by the heat, mum." This greatly relieved the troubled wife. "Oh, how did it happen?" she asked. "Well, you see, mum, he fell into a furnace at the foundry."

"NOT LIKELY"-Some years ago a rather unkempt traveller reached the Wivenhoe ferry and said to the boatman, "I'm broke, and I must get across the river. Will you trust me for a time?" "The fare is only a penny, mister," replied the ferryman, unmoved. "I know," said the hard up one, "but I havn't a ha'penny." "Mister," said the boatman, without the least sympathy, "if you ain't got a ha'penny, you won't be any better off on the other side than you are on this."

A SHADE OUT-Two young pupils were going to school in Colchester last week when their teacher passed them. "Just look at our teacher," said one, "she's got a white parasite," "Parasite!" echoed the other, "You mean parable." "Parable!" said the first. "Garn. That's what you fall out of an aeroplane with."

THE CLERGY-A motor-cyclist passing through Stanway stopped at a cottage gate where an old lady was standing, and asked to be directed to Bishop Stortford. She replied, "I am sorry; I don't know where he lives, but Canon Steele lives in the next village."

HONESTY-A wealthy visitor to a small village in Essex had been honouring the local confectioner's shop with her custom. As her chauffeur was taking her purchases to the car, she said to the little girl behind the counter. "It must be a great temptation for you ere, Don't you ever feel inclined to eat some of these nice cakes?" "Why, no, ma'am," she replied, in a shocked voice, "that would be stealing." I only gives each of 'em a lick now and again.

THE LIBERATOR-A few days ago I was walking down Osborne Street, Colchester, when a swarm of bees caught my attention in the doorway of the Old Bath Hotel, so I stood watching them. Presently an old lady came along, and seeing the swarm, said to me "Whatever are those, flies?" "No," I replied, "they are bees." "Good gracious," said the lady, "who ever let them out?"

DEFINITE PROOF- Mrs. Brown (to next door neighbour) : "Did your husband go to the club supper?" Mrs. Smith: "Oh yes, he went alright." Mrs. Brown: "And did he deliver his speech?" Mrs. Smith: "He must have done so, because he was speechless when he came home."
Blackheath.

ASKED FOR IT-A schoolmaster was lecturing to a class upon the circulation of the blood. "If I stand upon my head," said he, "the blood will run down to my head, will it not?" "Yes, sir," assented the boys. "Then," said the master, "why does the blood not run into my feet when I stand on my feet?" There was a pause for a few minutes, when a bright youth replied, "Please, sir, it's because your feet aint empty."
Colchester.

DUCKS-Since the opening of the new Bathing Place it appears that most of the women of Colchester are taking to swimming. This is the sort of girl to marry. Instead of getting a fellow over eyes and ears in debt by her extravagance, the darling would assist her husband in keeping his head above water.
Tiptree.

KNOTTY PROBLEM-Old Salt: "Yes, miss, we've some fine boats around here; some can steam twenty knots an hour." Young lady visitor: "Really! I suppose you steam the knots so the sailors can untie them easily?.
Colchester.

Old Salt: "Some boats can steam twenty knots an hour, Miss."
Young Lady Visitor: "Really! I suppose you steam the knots so the sailors can untie them easily."

NO REPLY-He dashed into the electrician's office, his face flushed with anger. "Didn't I ask you yesterday morning to send a man to mend our door bell?" he roared, "and didn't you promise to send round at once?" "But we did, sir," broke in the manager; "I'm quite sure of it." "Hi, Bill," he called to one of his workman, "didn't you go round to Park Lodge yesterday to do that job?" "Yes," replied Bill, "I went round alright, and I rang the bell for ten minutes, but I couldn't get an answer, so I guessed they must be all out."
Brightlingsea.

THE SAME WAY-A brother calling on his sister one morning went upstairs to see his niece, aged 3 years, in the nursery. After a few minutes her mother told her to show Uncle Dick the way down to the dining room. The child, turning to her uncle, said, "Which way did you come up, uncle?" "Up the stairs," "Well, that is the way down."
Great Horkesly.

THE EIGHTH WONDER-The recent owner of the second-hand car met the vehicle's present owner. "Car going well?" he inquired. "It's a wonder on hills," said the owner. The recent owner nodded in agreement. "I'm glad you have also found it so," he replied. "Yes," said the present owner, bitterly; "every time I come to one I wonder if it's going up."
Colchester.

OUR ANCIENT BURROW-My little girl, aged 8, came in so excited one day. "Oh, daddy, I've just heard the siren. It was a country call: it went like this" (making a noise like a siren). "That's right," said daddy . Now show me how it goes for the Borough. "Don't be so silly, daddy; they don't have fires in bunny-rabbit's holes, you know," was the answer daddy got.
Vouched for by A.G. Layer-de-la-Haye.

DID HE ENJOY IT?-The village cricket ground is used by all who care to subscribe, and heaps of our subscribers are boys attending school and those just left. While I was waiting in the pavilion with one or two others an Irish lad who had just left school came in. "Hallo, Philip," I said, "have you come along to get your eye in?" "Yes, Tom, I have. It's the first knock I've had this year and I havn't had that yet." Then it started to rain, and Philip,s knock, which he had had but didn't get, was further postponed.
West Bergholt.

DRAWN!-Great excitement was caused in a local office on Monday when the office boy came rushing in waving a telegram form and shouting "I've drawn a horse." He was immediately surrounded by the typists, who clamoured to see the form-on which they found a drawing of a horse.
Brightlingsea.

NO LAUGHING MATTER-It was dinner time at the Barracks. "Any complaints? 'asked the orderly officer. Private Simpkins jumped to his feet. "Yes, sir, I've got one," he said. "This Irish stew's funny." The officer stared hard at the man. "Funny?" he echoed, "then why aren't you laughing?"
Little Horkesley.

Didn't wish to get tipsy

REVOLUTIONIST-A Colchester lady who took her small son into a shop to buy fireworks was told by the proprietor that, as he had bought on a smaller scale this year, he was afraid that they would not go round. On hearing this the boy quickly put back the three Catherine wheels he had chosen and substituted crackers in their place.
Wivenhoe.

A QUESTION OF AGE-My brother was always proud because his birthday fell a day before his father's. Walking up High Street one day, a gentleman stopped him and said, "Well, my little man, and how old are you?" "I'm nine years old, sir." "Dear, dear." replied the gentleman, "You do surprise me." "Well," replied the boy," I think I ought to know; I'm a day older than my father."

THE END OF HIM-Choir Boy: "What made you give up singing in the choir?" Former colleague: "I was absent one Sunday, and somebody asked when the organ had been mended."
Colchester.

THE GOAT DID IT-I quite thought that Joe (who to be exact is rather a diminutive man) and Miss X. would make a match of it, but no, Joe declares that the thought of marriage terrifies him. It appears he arrived in Wivenhoe with cycle and side-car, to remove a dead goat from the home of Miss X. To use his own words:-"It was a confoundedly big goat, and dashed heavy, so you can imagine my surprise when Miss X. picked it up bodily and tossed it in the car as though it had been no more than a puppy." "What did you do?" I asked curiously. "Do?" said Joe. "Why made off, of course, before she served me the same."
Wivenhoe.

A BRIGHT IDEA-Some years ago before wireless was so popular and when "correct time" could only be obtained at the nearest railway station or town, a farmer living at an isolated farm near Great Oakley sent his farm yokel to Colchester market one Saturday with special instructions to bring back the correct time. The old man, before departing, looked at his watch to set it by the Town Hall clock, but found that the watch refused to resume duty. On his return his master said, "Well, John, did you bring the right time?" The old yokel produced a scrap of paper inscribed "5 past 3," and said "I wrote it down on this ere bit o'paper so I shouldn't forget it, as my watch had stopped.
Alresford.

THE VOICE AGAIN-"It's no good interrupting me," said a speaker at a Colchester out-door election gathering; "I'm a pretty old hand at this sort of thing." "You may be old," said a voice, "but you're not pretty."

A HOT ONE-My wife, who is addicted to the use of strong white peppermints as an aid to digestion, once gave one to my little girl, aged five. The child sucked the sweet for a moment, then hastily removed it from her mouth and placed it on the table. "Don't you like it?" asked my wife, "Yes, mummy," replied the child, "but I'm waiting for it to get cool."

DIDN'T WISH TO GET TIPSY-A man in a public-house had had more than was good for him. He said to his mate: "The very next time that 'ere door come round this way, I'll get up and go out."

West Mersea.

"The very next time that 'ere door come round this way, I'll go."

PERHAPS NOT-A candidate for the election, addressing his constituents in a local hall, was surprised by a voice shouting out from the back of the hall "I don't care wot you says, gov'nor; I wouldn't vote for you if you was the angel Gabriel." Quick as lightening came the reply "If I were the angel Gabriel you wouldn't be in my constituency."

TOUCHING THE SPOT-George, the Socialist labourer, was stating his views in support of his party, when one of his hearers asked "If you owned a thousand acres would you give me half ? "Yes," said George, "If you had a hundred pounds would you give me fifty" said another. "Ay, that I would," said George, with enthusiasm. "George," said his neighbour quietly, "If you had two pigs would you give me one?" "Ah!" replied George in an injured tone, "You know I've got two pigs."
Alresford.

THE WIRELESS EXPERT-I had installed a wireless set in my home and at first had only one pole with the other end of the aerial fastened to the house. Later, however, I procured another pole which I erected. A few days after this was a subject for comment amongst the neighbouring country-folk and the village "know-all" was explaining; "One pole is for England," he said, "and the other brings in France, but it would require many poles to get all stations." "Indeed," said a listener, "then what are double aerials for?" "Oh," replied know-all. "They are only for earphones."

MODERN BUSINESS METHODS-Two friends, who were both keen cyclists, were discussing their respective mounts. One of them possessed a new machine which was the type very popular in Colchester, and offered on generous terms by a large local dealer. His friend remarked, "I should have thought that you would have had something-er, well a little more uncommon than that," "Uncommon," was the indignant retort, "why in a sense it is absolutely unique-it's paid for!"
Colchester.

SMART BUSINESS-A woman had twopence; she went to a shop and got a loaf on tick; she sold the loaf for threepence; with the threepence and the twopence she went to the pictures.
Colchester.

Good for nothing

SAFETY FIRST-A candidate for parliamentary honours for a division in Essex was returning home one evening in his car when it broke down due to ignition trouble, the engine failing to fire at all. After effecting a temporary repair, he called a local farm labourer, asking him to hold a control while the owner made an attempt to start the engine. "Nunno," said the labourer, "not me; something might explode."

RESOURCEFUL-A certain young man in Colchester, having gained the promise of his lady friend, approached her father with a veiw to securing his daughter's hand in marriage. "I'm sure I don't know how you are going to manage it, my boy," said the father, after the young man had explained his purpose; "I can only just manage to keep her myself." "Oh, that's quite all right, sir," was the unabashed reply; "let us pool our resources."

DOING THE HEAVY-A gentleman living in Wivenhoe, was asked by his wife to drown a cat which was getting old and going blind. That evening at high tide he proceeded to the river and did the deed. On returning home his wife asked if he was sure that it was drowned and not swimming about the water and likely to get out and return home. "No, my dear," he replied; "it sank like a log and there is no chance of it coming to the surface again." "Why are you so sure?" asked the lady. "Because" answered the brute, "I tied a piece of your cake round its neck!"
Wivenhoe.

SAFETY FIRST-Both my boys have had chicken-pox, but the infectious period is now over. Seeing one of their little playmates going past the house the other day I asked her if she would like to come in the garden to play with Owen and Raymond. "No, I had better not," she replied, "because mother says they might still be affectionate!"
Wivenhoe.

MISTAKEN-During the recent holiday a lady friend of mine was travelling from Liverpool Station to Wivenhoe (LNER). Two or three other ladies were in the same carriage, one with a portmanteau, which she placed under the seat. On the way down a clergyman (of some denomination) entered the same carriage. The lady with the portmanteau had to change at one of the intermediate stations, when she asked the clergyman if he would mind passing her portmanteau along the carriage to her? His answer was, "Do you take me for a porter?" "No," said the lady, "I took you for a gentleman." The clergyman did not belong to Essex.
Wivenhoe.

GOOD FOR NOTHING-Johnnie: "Will you give me a penny, mother?" Mother: "What do you want it for?" Johnnie: "For being good all day." Mother: "Nonsense, Johnnie; can you not be good for nothing, like your father ?"
Colchester.

"A penny for being good all day"
"Can you not be good for nothing like your father?"

Nothing doing

RANK IGNORANCE-The orderly officer was going his rounds of the Barracks accompanied by the Orderly Sergeant, and entered one of the mess rooms where the men were having dinner. He asked the usual question "Any complaints?" where one of the men sprang to attention and said : "The 'spuds' ai'nt cooked properly, sir!" The officer asked the Sergeant what was meant by "spuds"? "Oh, that's his ignorance. Sir," said the Sergeant; "he means 'taters."

FED UP-A lady visitor to Wivenhoe was on the quay asking a fisherman all about how shrimps were caught and why and where. After about half-an-hour's questioning she said: "How many visitors do you get asking the same questions as mine during the summer?" "Two!" was the brief and crushing reply!
Wivenhoe.

A BRIGHT SUGGESTION-Two young men were discussing a fancy dress dance. "I don't know what to go as," remarked one ; "it's quite an informal affair, and will only be a small gathering." "A small gathering, did you say?" asked his friend. "Yes," was the reply. "Well," said the other, "why not go as a linseed poultice?"
Colchester.

AN EAR FOR BUSINESS-A concert was in progress in a village on the outskirts of Colchester. The final syllables of "The Village Blacksmith" had just died away to the accompaniment of applause, when a man came forward. "I've come round from the front," he said, "and I want you to do me a favour. I am the man you have been singing about, and next time I want you to put in a verse saying I also repair motor-bikes."
Bromley.

SUNDAY GAMES!-Johnny's parents were discussing what to give him for his birthday present when he decided to help them by suggesting a drum. "And mind," he said, "it's a Salvation Army drum." "Oh!" exclaimed his father, very much surprised, "Why a Salvation Army one in particular?" "Because then I can play it on Sundays," was the reply.
Colchester.

DISCONCERTING-The new typist at a large engineering firm in Colchester was an excellent typist, but not at all acquainted with engineering terms. On one occasion he was given the rough draft of a letter by his chief, who was notorious for his indistinct writing, which ran, "We are, therefore, sending you two pipes with brazed unions." Imagine the consternation of the chief when this was rendered: "We are, therefore, sending you two pints of braised onions."

NOTHING DOING-It was raining quite fast last Sunday night when a weary-looking tramp appealed to Mr.P., of Wivenhoe, who is noted for his hardness of heart "Yes, Sir," said the tramp, "I have seen better days." "So have I," replied Mr.P., as he closed the door; "but I believe the rain will do a lot of good!"

"I have seen better days sir"
"So have I, but I believe the rain will do a lot of good."

A LIGHT-WEIGHT-They sat opposite each other in a Colchester restaurant. One was a burly individual and the other a diminutive little man in a bowler hat. They had been steadily munching for a quarter of an hour, when the little man suddenly tapped the other on the arm. "Do you think you could pass me the sugar?" asked he, timidly. The burly one scowled and said, "Yes, I think I could; I've bin movin' pianners all me life."
Colchester.

EMBARRASSING OBEDIENCE-A teacher at a county school sent a small girl to get a pound of plums for sixpence, but told her to be sure and pinch one or two of them to see if they were ripe. Shortly afterwards the girl rushed in, breathlessly exclaiming, "Here, teacher, here's your sixpence; I pinched a whole bag-ful, but the man ain't far behind."

ANOTHER MARKET-An old countryman just home from the market at Colchester was telling his wife about the menagerie in High Street. "In High Street, same side as the Corn Exchange, that is," he said. "Why, silly," his wife exclaimed, "then that must be the Stock Exchange, with them bulls and bears you read about in the papers."

INTERESTING INFORMATION-We had just missed our bus, so we asked the driver of another how long the next bus would be. "Same as this one," he replied; "they're all the same size on that route".
Alresford.

EARLY EXPERIENCE!-When travelling to London on Saturday last the train stopped at Ingatestone, and a lady entered our carriage, accompanied by her little boy, aged about three. While waiting for the train to start the child looked out of the window and saw the signalman pulling over the levers in the signal box. Turning to his mother the innocent infant remarked: "Mummy! look at that man there drawing himself a pint!" Everybody laughed-excepting the mother.
Brightlingsea.

THE GUIDE SPIRIT-While aboard the Mersea-Bradwell motor launch the other day a small Guide, with a handful of orange peel, went up to the Captain and said "If you please, sir, may I throw this peel into the river?"
West Mersea.

"THIS EVENING TO FRESH WOODS"-Mother and child were against the Recreation Ground Bowling Green. "Come along now, Jackie; we must get home to tea." "I don't want to go, mummie," snivelled the youngster. "Yes, you must; come along now." Jackie began to cry and shake himself. Mother got cross and planted him firmly in the push-car. "There now, after tea you shall come back and see the funny old men throw them balls about.' Jackie was wheeled away without another whimper.

Part Two

Poem by Miss Gardner

In the following pages, I relate an event in 1823 which describes an account of a walk in Colchester taken by a Miss Europa Gardner with her mother to her friend Miss Yorke.

This is a rather long introduction to the good humoured lines which follow, in which there is only a faint vestige of politics. But it is necessary to realise the atmosphere of the period before reading the poem and to get some idea of the personages introduced therein.

The writer was a daughter of the Hon.H.W.Gardner presumably his eldest daughter, Miss Anne Europa Gardner. She was born probably about 1804. The Hon.H.W.Gardner who was married on February 20, 1803, being then 29, had five sons and five daughters. The eldest of the five sons was not born till August 19, 1815, and the youngest was born in May, 1827.

The dates of the births of the five daughters are not given but it appears that at least four of them were born before the eldest son. The poem given may be confidently attributed to Miss Anne Europa Gardner, afterwards Mrs. Gooch. The versification is clever and the descriptions of persons and incidents show considerable humour and literary skill.

Whilst professing to tell of a morning walk, it describes what must have been an afternoon excursion-about 2 p.m. to 4 p.m. It need not be supposed that all the incidents really took place in those two hours. Miss Gardner was writing to a friend at a distance and she took poetical licence, putting the experience of several days' walks into one letter. The lines are dated August, but she refers to St. Dennis' Fair, which was held always in October. She makes one personage say that the days are drawing in. She makes "Major Covell' remark: "Tis very bad weather, sad time for the hay,"

There are other discrepancies of date. But the general effect is extremely lively and her descriptions of over a score of the leading people of Colchester are most realistic. Miss Gardner's companion in her walk was her mother. To understand the personal allusions readers must refer to, the "WHO'S WHO," at the end which has been compiled as an addition to the poem.

Excitement about Queen Caroline

In 1820 took place, in the House of Lords, the divorce trial, in which unpleasant evidence was adduced against the Queen. She was charged with misconduct with one Bergami, whom she had employed as a courier in her long continental travel. She had shown great partiality to him and had obtained a foreign patent of nobility for him. She was proved to have behaved with indiscretion. The Bill for her divorce passed its third reading in the House of Lords by 108 to 99 votes. It was realised that in the House of Commons it would almost certainly be rejected and that outside Parliament there was danger of a revolution. The Bill was therefore dropped and the champions of the Queen triumphantly claimed that this was "an acquittal."

In those days if you were a Whig you believed in the Queen's innocence; if a Tory you believed in her guilt. George IV. had a bad reputation as a profligate and it was undeniable that he had behaved badly to Caroline. He was accordingly unpopular and the Queen became correspondingly popular. The Whigs embraced the popular side; the Tories stood by the King.

Address to King George IV. from Colchester

In Colchester feeling on the subject was high. In November, 1820, a fortnight after the Bill had been dropped when the country was excited by demonstrations in favour of Queen Caroline and attacks on King George IV, an address, signed by 93 inhabitants of Colchester, was sent to the Mayor (a Tory) desiring him to call a meeting "to consider the propriety of presenting an affectionate and loyal address to His Majesty, to evince our undiminished and unshaken Attachment to His Royal Person and Government; and our firm Determination to uphold by every means within our Power, our enviable Constitution in Church and State. The 93 signatories were all Tories:

They included: Lieut.-Col. COVELL, W. H. GARDNER, C. BOUTFLOWER, GORE BROWNE, S. DICKENS, H. HUTTON and JOHN DAKINS.

(It will be seen shortly why these names are picked out.) The meeting was held on November 27, 1820, when a glowing address to the King was passed unanimously and ordered to be sealed with the Borough Seal.

Illuminations in honour of Queen Caroline

But a week earlier some of the Whigs had issued a bill calling on the Colchester people to illuminate their houses on November 20th in honour of "the acquittal" of Queen Caroline.

As a counterblast a meeting was called "by requisition" to swear in Special Constables. The meeting took place at the Town Hall on November 20th and according to the report in the "Colchester Gazette," Gore Browne, Esq., "with the approbation of the meeting" proposed that all present enrol themselves as Special Constables, to preserve the peace, but not (as the Mayor explained) to prevent people illuminating their houses, "if they thought proper.

Amongst those enrolled were: The Hon. W. H. GARDNER DANIEL S. TREVOR DICKENS Esq. CHAS BOUTFLOWER, Esq. JOSEPH BENWELL, Esq. DANIEL O.BLYTH, Esq.. THOMAS GORE BROWNE, Esq. RICHARD COVELL, Esq.. Esq THOMAS TAYSPILL. [Again the sequel will explain the selection of those names.]

The Whigs, or some of them, illuminated their houses. "The Colchester Gazette" (November 25, 1820), strongly against Queen Caroline, scoffed at these illuminations,-"a third edition of rushlight brilliancy." A list given of the illuminated houses included those of the Rev. Mr. Starns, Mr. Firmin, Mr. Wilmshurst (Head Street) and "premises in Head Street over the shop of Mr. Paul Aggio"—who wrote next week an indignant letter—published in the "Colchester Gazette"—stating that he displayed no sort of illumination and that the premises over his shop were not occupied by him..

Curious specimen of Journalism

Both sides seem to have been absurdly excited. On December 9, 1820, the "Colchester Gazette" contained this remarkable specimen of editorial fervour, which might have inspired Charles Dickens, a few years later in his account of journalism at Eatanswill:

Although we write with gunpowder beneath us-although the finger of malignity points at us, the tongue of infamy traduces, and the coward holds under a mask his poisoned dart at our throat, we calmly pursue the duteous task, unmoved by their power, but with pity for their meanness....But the spell is nearly past; the cloud nearly dispersed. Truth, over-awing Truth, bursts from the reflecting mind, and, as she rises, the veil of delusion vanishes."

All which was supplementary to a violent editorial attack on the morals of Queen Caroline and an equally vehement defence of the virtues of George IV.

Miss Gardners poetical epistle to Miss York

Account of a walk in Colchester in the early 1800s

In 1823, Colchester was buzzing with some very amusing gossip. The following poem, written by a young lady, Miss Anne Europa Gardner, (Late Mrs. Gooch), was the daughter of the Lieutenant General H.W.Gardner who had ten children, five sons and five daughters. From 1820 to 1823, and perhaps longer, he lived with his numerous family at the Hythe, Colchester, within the sound of the church clock, (presumably, St. Leonard's) and not far from the Colchester barracks, which at that time, existed somewhere on the south side of Magdalen Street.

He must have required a very large house. It seems to have been called "Belle Vue". This may identify it if it still exists. But more likely it was one of the officer's houses which were afterwards demolished on the south side of what is now called Barrack Street.

Writing to her dear friend, Miss Yorke in the year 1823, she describes a walk in Colchester with her mother, from Water Lane, (Brook Street) Colchester, through the town, and into the countryside. She describes the acquaintances that she encountered throughout the journey, and the gossip that ensued.

The Poem

To *Miss Yorke.*

We purpos'd one morning, a beautiful day
Our friend *Mrs. Cuming* a visit to pay;
Our things we put on without waiting to talk,
And now I will give an account of our walk.
You're not to suppose we met anything new
To us, though twill certainly be so to you,
Accustom'd to beautiful woods, hills and dales,
And not often troubled with Country Town tales.
We set off, but just as we got to the door,
We met *Mr. Parry* with one or two more,
Miss Elizabeth Tayspill and good *Mr. Blythe,*
So we joined with the Party just come from the Hythe.
At the corner we parted for they chose the street,
But we who had tender regard for our feet,
Went down Water Lane, which you very well know
Is the way to the Town that we most often go.
We now hasten'd on at so rapid a pace,
You might almost suppose we were running a race.
At the end of the Lane, *Parson Huit* we meet,
Whom we both with a *bow* condescended to greet.
This Parson for learning is very much fam'd,
But his *preaching* and practice are equally blam'd.
He's a mortal dislike to the Family Roy'l,
And the prayer for His Majesty always will spoil,
And contrive by some trick with an artful grimace
To turn the whole family out of their place.
East Hill now appears, which as we ascend,
Our pace I assure you we dont try to mend,
For if *down hill,* we seem to be running a race,
We always go *up* at a funeral pace.
We heard a great shouting, and found 'twas the Mayor.
Or rather his herald, proclaiming the fair,
The bells began ringing, the day was so fine,
That to mirth, joy and pleasure all seem'd to incline.
The *Dobson's* and *Dalon's* as usual grace
Their windows with many a sweet looking face.
Now with a quick step come one after us run;
'Twas gay *Mr. Benwell* enjoying the fun;
He very much press'd us to go home and dine,
To eat toasted cheese, and to drink elder wine;
But as they expected us home in an hour,
To comply with his wishes was out of our pow'r.
He was going our way, so onward we walk'd,
But really 'twas shameful to hear how we talk'd.
"*Mrs. Mackintosh* ails with a fit of the spleen.
"Why? *Miss Gurdon* (*Gordon* altered in a
later hand to *Gurdon*) has call'd in *Sir Lachlan Maclean,*

"And poor Dr Mac. who long thought she look'd ill,
"Had flatter'd himself that a calomel pill,
"Just given in time, with some leeches applied
"To her chest and her temples, perhaps to her side.
"And a few *harmless draughts,* with soft manners to please,
"Would entitle him surely, to take twenty fees.
"But his castles are fallen, and then his poor wife,
"Says she never felt anything so in her life,
"Though *that* cry in *Colchester's* rather too stale,
"As she most days finds need to repeat the same tale,"
We had much more to say but now 'twas our luck,
To meet *Mr. Martin,* a very great buck,
Who taking his friend *Mr. Benwell* away,
Put a stop to our converse, and wish'd us good day.
We soon observe Show Carts, slow moving along,
Birds, Beasts, Dwarfs and Giants all mix'd in a throng;
Our gracious Queen Caroline, lying in state,
With all her attendants, lamenting her fate;
There was Lady Anne Hamilton, Bergami too,
Austin, Alderman Wood, and the rest of the crew,
What a glorious sight! in wax representation,
And shewn at half price for the good of the nation*
We now enter High Street, so broad and so gay,
Where we meet beaux and belles, all in splendid array;
Miss Mills's so elegant walk in a row,
With the *Huttons* and *Hoblins* to make up the show.
But lo! now before us a figure appears,
Who you'd think was approaching the Dey of Algiers;
His looks are so *awe-struck,* his bow so profound,
That his head and his feet almost meet on the ground;
A few steps he advances with wondrous grace,
Another deep bow, with the same pompous face;
We now meet and shake hands, but my muse must run faster,
And name him as *Covell,* the great Barrack Master,
From the reading room fresh Major Covell was come,
It was not then in reason to think he'd be mum,
So we both stood prepar'd for the news of the day,
Whether birth, death or marriage, ball, concert or play,
With an awful long face then, the Major begins
In a whisper to talk of notorious sins;
"Sad news in the Town, *Miss Anne Round* is run off
"With *Mr. John Thompson,* that little black dwarf;
"Her father's enrag'd beyond measure they say,
"And would have pursued without any delay,
"But which way they're gone, not a soul can find out,
"As they've manag'd to cut off all trace of their route,
"Tis very bad weather, sad time for the hay,
"My compliments, Ma'am, to the Colonel I pray."
Thus he bow'd and we parted quite glad to escape,
From further partic'lars respecting this scrape.

We just stopped at *Nashes*, to order some chickens,
When who should pop in, but good *Mrs. Sam Dickens,*
Who begg'd us to stay for a minute or two,
As she'd walk'd till she'd put herself quite in a stew.
Mrs. Holt (she went on) gave a party last night,
Which went off but stupidly, as it well might;
The party, they tell me, assembled by eight,
And a terrible time Mrs. Holt made them wait,
Ere she made her appearance, and then she came down
In a gold spangled turban, and high morning gown,
The party all sat round the room in due form,
As silent as Cattle expecting a storm;
At length some one ventur'd the novel remark,
How short the days grow, ma'am, how soon it gets dark!
Indeed, Sir. it does,-then a long pause ensues,
Which is broken by some body's asking the news.
Mrs. Holt now goes round, in the usual way,
To beg if the tea does not suit they will say;
Pray a little more sugar, I take my tea sweet;
Your cream is so good ma'am, 'tis really a treat,
Miss Dobson, I hope you have all that you wish;
I'll trouble you, ma'am, for another half-dish.
With converse like this the party was cheer'd,
Till the time when the cloaks and the pattens appear'd.-
We now felt impatient, to push on our way-
So we civilly bid Mrs. Dickens good day,
And as we had still our visit to make,
We thought 'twould be wisest a short cut to take;
So we hasten'd along at the back of the town,
Where we met not a creature save *Capt'n Gore Brown,*
But as it grew late, we had not time to stay,
So we bow'd, and pass'd on without further delay.
It's well that we did so, for if we had not,
He'd have kept us an hour, with accounts of his yacht.
Which yacht, by the bye, it is very well known,
Is merely a hired one, none of his own.
At our friends now arriv'd, we hop'd to have pass'd
A short time quite quietly with her at last;
But fate was determin'd to tease us to-day,-
We scarce were set down, and all much to say,
When the door was bounc'd open and who should appear,
But the fam'd *Mr. Boutflower,* known far and near?
Now after the usual greetings were o'er,
Teeth well pick'd, head well scratch'd, and
he'd spit on the floor,
He felt our friends pulse, which I'm happy to say,
He pronounced to be very much better to day;
For all the world speaks of his medical skill,
Though rather too fond of the calomel pill.
He'd just commenc'd telling among other tales

Of an excellent dinner he gave *Mr. Bales;*
He meant to enumerate every dish,
But had not got beyond the soup, Patties and Fish
When a very loud screaming was heard below stairs;
To the window we ran and saw two dancing bears,
But 'twas not from them, that the screams seem'd to come
Indeed the poor creatures were forc'd to keep dumb;
So down Mr. Boutflower flew like a shot
I *follow'd* and there danced *Miss Helme* on the spot.
She screamed her own time, and kept time with the bear,
Which had frighten'd her senses all into the air-
Mr. Boutflower at last got her out of the street
And we brought her up stairs, looking pale as a sheet,
But she quickly recover'd, and when she got right;
She ask'd us what secrets she'd told in her fright,
And when we assured her, not one whatsoever,
Her converse, as usual, was very clever.
But now, as Miss Emily Gascoigne was there,
And herself and Miss Helme were a suitable pair,
We took leave of our friends and reach'd the hall door
Exact as the Hythe clock began to strike four.
Papa prais'd us greatly for scraping our shoes,
And Mama and myself repeated the news.
And now my dear girl, with abhorrence you'll shrink
If I candidly say to you, which do you think
The most entertaining amusement will yield,-
A walk in the town, or a ride in the field ?

The "Who's Who" of the Poem

MR. BALES.-This is the Rev. Philip Bayles, who, at this time, was rector of St. Mary-at-the-Walls, Colchester, a popular and prominent parson. Mr. Boutflower was one of his chief parishioners and it is natural that he should have asked his rector, as he says, to dinner, at 61, Crouch Street.

MR. BOUTFLOWER.-Charles Boutflower, Esq. "lived at 61, Crouch Street, the old Georgian mansion demolished in 1931 to provide a site for the Regal Theatre. Mr. Boutflower was one of the three honorary surgeons to the Colchester Hospital in 1825. He was also one of the Committee (1825) of the Colchester and Essex Botanical and Horticultural Society. He was medical attendant to Mrs. Cuming."

MR. BENWELL.-"Gay Mr. Benwell," who pressed Miss Gardner and her mother to dine with him on toasted cheese and elder wine, is described as a gossip and chatterbox. He is no doubt the "Joseph Benwell, Esq.," who enrolled a special constable with the Hon. W. H. Gardner and the rest, but there is no clue to his occupation.

CAPT. GORE BROWN.-This is the Gore Browne, who was prominent as a special constable in 1820. His full name seems to have been Thomas Gore Browne. Son or relative of Stephen Browne of the Hythe and Wivenhoe, a well-to-do merchant and ship-owner. Stephen Browne seems to have had a residence in Crouch Street.

Artist, Major John Bale's picture of St Leonards Church at the Hythe, Colchester

MR. BLYTHE."Good Mr. Blythe" was undoubtedly "Daniel O. Blythe, Esq.," a ship-owner at the Hythe, one of the special constables sworn in with the Hon. H. W. Gardner in November, 1820. He was one of the five Trustees of the Colchester and Essex Botanical and Horticultural Society (1823). He was a member ("assistant") of the Colchester Corporation. Evidently a man of position and substance.

COVELL.-"The great Barrack Master." This is "Lieut-Colonel Covell," who was one of the 93 Tory signatories in November, 1920. "Richard Covell, Esq., "Sworn in the following week as a special constable was probably his son. Miss Garner calls him "Major Covell" and makes fun of his exaggerated bowing and scraping. The reading-room from which he had arrived was No. 56 High Street, the premises of the "Colchester Library", founded in 1803. Liptons' shop now occupies the site. "The Colonel," to whom Covell sends his compliments, means Lieut.-Colonel the Hon. H. W. Gardner.

MRS. CUMING.-Probably a mis-spelling for "Cumming" (an old Scottish family). she appears to have lived on the other side of Colchester, some way from the Hythe. Perhaps her name, introduced as "our friend Mrs. Cuming" was familiar to Miss Yorke." Mrs. Cuming (Lucy Margaret, nee Yorke) wife of George Cumming, M. D. (m. May, 1814), was sister of Peirce Wynne Yorke, of Co. Denbigh, Wales (High Sheriff, 1817), and also of Miss Diana Yorke, who would have been 29 or 30 in 1823. She died unmarried in 1855, aged 72. There is no evidence, however, that Dr. Geo. Cumming was ever connected with Colchester nor does the name of "Mrs. Cuming" occur in any Colchester records or directories of c. 1823.

THE DAKENS.-The Rev. John Dakins, M. A., rector of St. James, Colchester, lived on East Hill.

MRS. SAM DICKENS.-This breathless and talkative lady was wife of "Samuel Trevor Dickens, Esq.,"one of the special constables enrolled in 1820.

THE DOBSONS.-Of doubtful identity. Ann Dobson was a milliner and dress-maker in St. Botolph's Street (1839).

MISS GARDNER.-Miss Anne Gardner, eldest daughter of Lieut. General the Hon. H. W. Gardner. Born about 1804; married February 20, 1829, Captain Thomas Sherlock Gooch, R. N. third son of Sir Thomas Sherlock Gooch, 5th Baronet, of Benacre Hall, Suffolk. She died September 8, leaving issue.

MISS SUSAN GARDNER.-Sister of the presumed author of the poem, and third daughter of the Hon. H. W. Gardner. She married, March 14, 1830, Lieut. John James, 90th Light Infantry, From the lines addressed to her on her birthday July 1, 1826, when she was probably about 20 or 21 years old, she seems to have had "mental light" and "loveliness of soul," as well as a share of beauty in the usual sense. Her husband, said to have been of Shelford, Cambridgeshire, is apparently the Captain John James, 90th Light Infantry," who published in 1879," Mesmerism: with Hints for Beginners."

MISS EMILY GASCOIGNE.-Not identified. She was a visitor or a resident at "Mrs. Cuming's" house, and apparently was known to Miss Yorke, to whom the poem was written.

MISS GURDON.-Originally written "Miss Gordon." "J. Gurdon, Esq." one of the vice-Presidents of the Colchester Philosophical Society in 1825, was presumably John Gurdon, of Assington Hall (b. 1791). He had a sister Miss Jermima Gurdon, who was probably the wealthy patient who disappointed Dr. Macintosh's hopes by calling in his rival, Sir Lachlan Maclean, M.D.

MISS HELME.-Visitor to Mrs. "Cuming." This hysterical lady, gifted as a conversationalist, is not identified. **THE HOBLINS.**-The Rev. Richard Hoblyn, M.A. was rector of All Saints' with St. Botolph's, Colchester. He was (in 1825) one of the Library Committee (of five) of the Castle Society, a rather exclusive literary circle in Colchester. At this period the parish church of St. Botolph was in ruins and disused.

MRS HOLT.-This lady who gave a party which was dull in spite of the fact that she wore a gold spangled turban and high morning gown, Dr. G. P. Holt, a physician, was one of the four vice-presidents (in 1825) of the Colchester Philosophical Society for the Promotion of Scientific and Literary Pursuits, "established May 3, 1820. The Society had a house in Queen Street, with lecture room, and a small library and a quaintly assorted museum.

PARSON HUIT.-The Rev. Charles Hewitt, rector of Greenstead, to which he was inducted in 1794. He held the living for about 50 years. He was a Whig, and no doubt a champion of the "Injured Queen."

THE HUTTONS.-The Rev. H. Hutton D. D., was rector of Mile End. He was one of the 93 Tory signatories who asked in November 1820 for a meeting to be called in support of the King. Constitution, Church and State, etc.

MRS. MACKINTOSH.-Wife of "R.D.Mackintosh, Esq., M.D., "one of the four vice-presidents of the Colchester Philosophical Society. Mrs. Mackintosh was greatly perturbed because an important and wealthy patient, of her husband, Miss Gurdon, had called in Sir Lachlan Maclean, physician, who had thus superseded Dr. Mackintosh.

SIR LACHLAN MACLEAN.- Sir Lachlan Maclean, Knight, M.D., who lived at the Hythe, Colchester, was (in 1825) one of the vice-presidents of the Colchester and Essex Botanical and Horticultural Society, which established the Botanical Gardens on land at the back of Grey Friars, East Hill. The Society was formed on July 3, 1823.

MR. MARTIN.-"A very great buck" and a friend of the "gay" Mr. Benwell. Mr. Samuel J. Edgell Martin was an attorney in Colchester in 1825. It is probably he or his son that is here mentioned.

THE MISS'S MILLS.-Daughters of Mr. John Fletcher Mills, banker of Lexden Park, High Sheriff of Essex in 1839, son of Mr. John Mills, founder of the bank afterwards Mills Errington Bawtree and Co. There were three Miss Mills,- Fanny who married, November 23, 1824, George Henry Errington, banker, afterwards of Lexden Park (he died 1883); Elizabeth, who seems to have died unmarried; and Hester Ann, who married September 1832, the Rev. Wm. Wilson.

NASHES.-James Nash, dealer in game and fishmonger, had a shop in Middle Row, Colchester, the row of houses at the east end of St. Runwald's church, extending nearly to opposite the Red Lion Hotel.

MR. PARRY.-The Rev. Thomas Parry was rector of the Hythe Church (St. Leonard's).

MISS ANNE ROUND.- Eliza Ann Round, who, we are glad to know, married John Ringler Thomson ("Mr. John Thomson") in 1823, was sister of George Round of East Hill House (d. 1857). whose portrait is in Colchester Town Hall, and was aunt of the late Mr. Edward Augustus Round, of St. Peter's, Colchester, and of Lexden House (d. November 14, 1823, aged 51) She was grand-daughter of James Round of Birch Hall (d. 1806). She had two sons and died February 28, 1869.

St Runwald's Church and Middle Row High Street, in 1857.
Site of Nashes (James) dealer in game and fishmonger.

MISS ELIZABETH TAYSPILL.- This lady was born in Colchester in 1801. After her father's death in 1831 she removed to St. John's Wood, and she died unmarried in 1887, aged 86. She was daughter of Thamas Tayspill, of St. Leonard's parish, The Hythe, Colchester. Thomas Tayspill was Collector of Customs at the Custom House, The Hythe. He was a member (assistant) of the Colchester Corporation and was highly respected. He died April 18, 1831, aged 59, and was buried in St. Leonard's churchyard, where there is a stone inscribed in his memory. He was one of the last descendants of the Protestant Refugee family of Tayspill, which settled in Colchester c. 1600, coming from Ypres and Neuve Eglisc to escape persecution. Thomas Tayspill was son of Peter Tayspill, burgess of Colchester, weaver. The Tayspill's were distantly related to the Round family, of Birch Hall, and to the Rebow's.

MR. JOHN THOMPSON.-This "little black dwarf" was Mr. John Ringler Thomson, who married Miss Ann Round on April 20, 1823. He died February 28, 1869. The date of the marriage shows that the conversation could hardly have taken place (as alleged) in August, 1823.

MISS YORKE.-This lady cannot be identified with certainty. We are told that she was accustomed to beautiful woods, hills and dales. "As she is addressed by Miss Gardner as "my dear girl" she must have been of about the same age. She is twitted with a preference for a "ride in the field." She might have been a sister of Peirce Wynne Yorke, of Denbigh, Wales, but this is entirely conjectural.

Evidently Miss Yorke had been previously a visitor (to the Gardners ?) at Colchester for she "very well knew" Water Lane(Brook Street). Probably also she knew some of the persons alluded to. Otherwise the letter would not have had much point as far as she was concerned.- See Mrs. Cuming" in the Who's Who'.

* This is a description of the Fair caravans making their way to High Street, including a wax-work show, "Queen Caroline Lying in State, Lady Ann Hamilton was the Queen's Lady in Waiting and accompanied the Queen's corpse to Colchester and to Harwich in 1821. Bergami was the Italian courier, already mentioned as Queen Caroline's favourite. "Austin" is William Austin, another favourite servant of Queen Caroline, superseded by Bergami. Alderman Wood was Sir MatthewWood, M.P. for London and ex-Lord Mayor the Queen's most enthusiastic champion. He was grandfather of the late F.M. Sir Evelyn Wood.

Part Three

Essex Ballads

CHARLES EDWIN BENHAM.

Illustrated by

ANDREW DODDS

COLCHESTER 1996

First published 1895
A limited edition of Essex Ballads was printed for private distribution to friends only, of Benham and Company in 1960.

Preface

CHARLES BENHAM'S *Essex Ballads* were first published just over one-hundred years ago as Essex Ballads and Other Poems, with a foreword by The Right Honourable the Countess of Warwick who, in writing to Mr. Benham said of his work, and I quote, Besides a very considerable skill in versification, you have handled local dialect in such a way as will tend helpfully to perpetuate many archaic and interesting forms of folk speech.

Throughout your book I have found what should, I think, be in every local volume, a very welcome note of homeliness, the love of home and the love of one,s own county. After reading "ESSEX BALLADS" I am sure the book will be of much use and great popularity in the county villages.
FRANCIS EVELYN WARWICK.

The book which was a tremendous success was immediately taken to the hearts of the people of north Essex, its popularity was so great that it was republished seven times before becoming out of print during the Second World War, this new edition is the first since 1935 to be made available to the general public.

Essex Ballads by Charles Edwin Benham and illustrated by Andrew Dodds, a dweller of the Tendring Hundred was however, reissued by Benham Newspapers Limited as a very special limited edition in 1960 and was produced for private distribution only to friends of Benham and Company.

Charles Benham was editor and part proprietor of the Essex County Standard, the responsibility for which he shared with his elder brother, Sir Gurney Benham, compiler of the classic Benham's Book of Quotations. Charles Benham however, was the more retiring of the two often preferring a visit to the nearby woods to study the birds and flowers before starting his days work at the office. He also wrote weekly for forty-five years for the Essex County Standard, a column of charmingly quizzical 'Colchester Jottings' under the pseudonym of Mark Downe. His interests were far and wide ranging from mesmerism, pin-hole cameras, spectroscopes, and the for-runner of our present day radio's, the crystal radio set. His dry pile battery, which rang a bell for many years without attention, and his harmonograph machine, which drew diagrams through the swinging of two pendulums, are preserved in the Colchester Holly Trees Museum.

Charles Benham was a man who appreciated everything around him and his thoughts would often dwell on the wondrous ways of God and of man. He joined the Church of Rome towards the end of his life.
At Easter, 1929, at the age of sixty-nine, he had been in retreat at Roehampton. Returning on the Monday afternoon he went straight to his office and that night was found dead in his editorial chair.
The Essex Ballads have been described as the best dialect poetry ever written, they certainly give the reader a true and accurate description of life in those early days.

J.M.H.

Contents

Essex Ballads

Page

"Master go'n be sowd"
(A ballad of astonishment)

MASTER ha' gone to the Court! An' the farm an' the stock to be sowd!
Well, I am wholly amaized. I was here at eleven year owd-
That'll be forty-two year, come Michaelmas next-an' you say
Master ha, gone to the Court! What, an' brok' because he carn pay?

Things must be wunnerful bad, do master 'ad never ha' broke,
Him as olluz a sight o' good luck, why that seem like a joke.
Master gone to the Court? What an' filed his petition an' that?
Ten years agao I'd as soon ha' believed it as eaten my hat.

An' wha's go'n to come o' the land-three hund'd o' acres an' more?
Wha's go'n to come o' the land? Tha's a go'n to be sowd ? But good lor,
Who is the fule of a chap tha's goin' to buy it, I say?
Land that 'ont pay, to be sowd? Yes, but who is a goin' to buy?

An' wha's go'n to come o' we chaps? Are we all going straight to the House?
What, me an' Tom Hodge, an' Jack Wilson, an' Harry, an' Sandy, an' Rous
Along o' the master an' missus? Good lor, man alive, if we must
I knaow, when we git there, together, I knaow I shall larf till I bust.
"The lan' for the people! "Old Warty, he talk to 'em wunnerful grand,
But wha's go'n to come o' the people, and wha's go'n to come o' the land?

Well, that is the master bit I do think I ever was tow'd.
What is go'n to come o' this country if Master's a go'n to be sowd?

"Miss Julia: The Parsons daughter"
(A ballad of Love)

I LOIKE to watch har in the Parson's pew
A Sundays, me a settin' in the choir;
She look jest wholly be'utiful, she do.
That fairly sim to set my heart a-fire.

Her gowden hair, a-glist'rin in the sun,
Them bright blew eyes-good lor, I see 'em now!
I carn abear it when the sarmon's done,
That fare to make me feel I dunner how.

Las' Saddy, I was 'long o' Tom and Bill,
Down on th' allotment, back o' Thompson's Farm,
When she come past us, walkin' tard the hill,
A basket of them paigles on her arm.

'Nice evenin', John', she say, as she goo by,
An' smiled-goodstruth, you mighter knock' me down.
'That is indeed, Miss', I was go'n to say,
But there, I couldn't, give me 'arf-a-crown.

Says Bill, a-larfin', as she tarned the lane,
'She's waiting for yer, round the corner, bor',
I give 'ee sich a look, he larft again,
And made me feel that mad I could a swore.

I carnt abide it when these bits o' chaps
Talk of Miss Julia, saime as if they might
If she was some bloke's gal, but lor, prehaps
I think too much o' har, a jolly sight.

That sim ridic'lous nons'nse this, I doubt,
A tellin' on yer how she make me feel,
But who's to help it when she walk about
More like a angel than a gal a deal ?
That made me wild to see that Lunnon chap,
What come down to the Hall las' Mon'ay week,
A-coaxin' o' the dawg there in her lap,
She settin' in the garden-dang his cheek.

But there, Miss Julia! Lawk a mussy me,
I didn't oughter think of har n' more.
That aint as if she know I cared for she,
And do I reckon she'd give me what for.

"There's olluz summat"
(A ballad of wrath)

THERE'S olluz summat. When tha's wet
The corn git laid, the hay git sp'iled,
And when tha's dry the lan' git set.
That fare to make me wholly riled.

Look there, together, goodalive,
Them chick'ns send me fairly wild.
See them a-scrappin' in the drive?
That fair to make me wholly riled.

Why carn Tom shet gaites like he should?
He aint got no more sense 'n a child.
A-talkin' aint a mite o' good-
That fare to make me wholly riled.

Now wha's that kid a-cryin' for?
Look, Emma, carnt you hold that child?
Here, drat this pipe, why 'ont it dror?
That fare to make me wholly riled.

That rain again. How that do rain!
Here, Mary, aint them taters biled?
You're olluz half an hour behin',
That fare to make me wholly riled.

Hark how that blaow; jes what I thought,
That barley field 'll all be sp'iled.
A Saddy's moon is good for naught-
That fare to make me wholly riled.

You want it wet, tha's olluz fine,
You want it cowd, tha's olluz mild,
You want it dry, there's nought but rain,
That fare to make me wholly riled.
There's olluz summat; if 'taint that
Its tother-fare to drive yer wild.
Don' matter tuppence what yer at,
Things olluz make yer wholly riled.

"I din knaow"
(A ballad of politics)

Warty, he talk to 'em to-rights las' night-
I never h'ard a chap a talkin' sao.
He say the lan' an' that is ourn by right'
But bless yer, I din knaow.

He say we're all a poor deown-trodden lot,
A set o' slaives-tha's fact he towd us sao.
He say we oughter hev I dunner wot,
But bless yer, I din knaow.

Good night! He give it to our Parson str'ight-
I reck'n if tha's right he'll hev to gao.
The Charch an' taithe are ourn, he say, by right,
But bless yer, I din knaow.

I olluz sorter liked our Parson; thought
He wornt at all a bad un as the' gao,
Yet Mister Warty say I didn't ought,
But bless yer, I din knaow.

Las' winter, when my poor owd missus died,
Parson he come to see us through the snaow.
Old Warty say that's on'y cos he's paid,
But bless yer, I din knaow.

He simd right kind to me and my booy Bob;
He sent us meat and things-a reg'lar shaow.
Goodstruth, our Parson! Who'd a thought he'd rob?
Well bless yer, I din knaow.

And Mister Warty, 'cordin' as it seems,
He bin our fri'nd these years and years agao,
A warkin' out for everlastin' schemes,
But dang it, I din knaow.

The las' elecsh'n when them yallers found
I wear'd a bit o' blew, they say "Hulloa,
You aint a go'n to wote for Mr. Round ? "
But I says, I din knaow.

Tha's what I olluz tell 'em when they praite,
I carnt abear these chaps wot cackle sao.
That fairly stop their jawin', don't maite?
Jes tell em-You din knaow.

"Them haunted housen"
(A ballad of warning)

GOO' mornin', sir, you minter say you bought them housen there,
An' you're a-go'n ter live in one? Well, that'll make 'em stare.
Them housen, sir, is harnted, an' was when I's a lad,
An' anyone as sleep there sir, is sartin to be had.

I wouldn't tell yer, but surelie, I knaow as you'll repent.
Tek my advice, sir, don't you gao, y'll on'y wish yer hent,
Tha's no good you a-larfin, don't you sleep 'ithin that plaice.
Do to-night you'll be a-larfin on the wrong side o' yer faice.

There's jes one thing about it, you 'ont want to be there long
Afore you say my wahrd is right, though now you think tha's wrong.
The rets? Nao, sir, that ent the rets, n'r yet the moice, I guess.
But tha's the Owd un, I believe, an' nothin' more n'r less.

Las' night I passed them housen by, along o' Tom an' Jack.
"There'll be a tempest, booy," I say, "the moon lay on her back."
The wind were flanny, an' the clouds come up as black as slaites,
An' soon that lightened crost the sky, an' thundered jes to rights.

You oughter sin them winders, sir, all lit o' fire-good luck!
And rattled-I sh'd think th' did-my stars, them winders shuk!
We didn't stop. I tell yer why, we felt that dreffful bad,
Afear the Owd un sh'd come out, an' we sh'd a bin had.

Ah' you can larf, but don't you lay your head 'ithin that plaice.
Do to-morrer you'll be larfin on the wrong side o' yer faice.
Them housen, sir, is harnted, an' was since I's a lad-
Tek my advice, sir, don' you gao-yer sartin to be had.

"Little Jimmy King'om-come"
(A ballad of persecution)

What, remember little Jimmy? I should rather thinker do.
How we use ter plaigue his life out! Why, I never rightly knew.
But there, the booy was darft, yer knaow, an' olbut deaf an' dumb,
An' we olluz used ter call him little Jimmy King'om come.

He rowled off a hay stack onst, acrost a iron bin,
An' that onsensed him for a week; he ne'er was right agin.
He simd a loikely child afore-a smart, quick-witted brat,
But arter that ere fall he got as pudden-brined as that.

He'd set a gahpin' on a gaite all by hisself for hours,
Or a-wandrin' long the hedge-raows, gath'rin lots o' cultch an' flowers,
He was olluz up to sumfin, an' 'twas olluz sumfin rum,
Why, everybody knaowed him, little Jimmy King'om come.

Little Jim was that soft-hearted that he wouldn't hart a flea.
I've h'ard 'em say the sparrers wornt a mite afraid o' he;
An' anyhow I sin the bards a feedin' from his hand-
Tha's fact, though why they wornt afeared I ne'er could unnerstand.

I recollec' how me an' Bill, one Sunday, dinner time,
Found little Jimmy fas' asleep, his little basket by'm-
The little cob his mother olluz use ter let him taike,
With some bread and cheese inside it, or a bit of harvest caike.

Well, me an' Bill, we et it all, without a-waikin he,
An' then Bill give the booy a shaike. That was a master spree.
To see him lookin' for the caike. I p'inted to a shrub,
A maikin' signs to let him think a bard had et the grub.

At farst you should a sin him look, and harf begin to cry.
But when he saw the black-b'd there his faice was lit o' j'y.
He din care then. He thought that bard had taiken every crumb-
He was a caution, that ere booy, that Jimmy King'om come.

I recollec', one evenin' time, we tied him to a tree,
An' made belief the ghaost ud come at dark an' gobble he;
An' Jack come roun' at midnight with a sheet acrost his back,
An' olbut skeered him in a fit-a reglar tease was Jack.

We let him gao, all shaikin' hom', an' olbut dead o' fright,
A scamprin' 'long the laine there, in the middle o' the night.
Goodstruth, to see young Jimmy runnin'! Lor, you woulder larft.
"Onkoind?" You talk like Parson, sir, why lor, the booy was darft!

You talk jest how our Parson talked; yer make me call to mind
The times an' times he use to tell us "teasin' wasn't kind."
"Pray let em be," he used to say, but lor, we on'y larft-
A funny thing he didn't sim to see the booy was darft.

An' Jimmy's mother, too, my stars, we use ter maike har riled.
She'd nilly cry her eyes out over that ere bloomin' child.
Them women! Wha's the good o' talkin' to them? Not a mite.
But there, she shooly mighter sin as how the booy warnt right.

But what was I a tellin' on yer?-Ah, about the ghaost.
He died about a fortnight arter that-a month at moast.
We used ter give he beans, we did. Goodnight, you woulder larft.
That do sim, as you say, a shaime, but there, the booy was darft.

"Jim's new gal"
(A ballad of jealousy)

WHO'S he got there? Good lawk, if that ain't Sal-
Har that's at wark at Rob't Wilson's farm.
There's no mistaike, this time he's got a gal:
Jes see 'em, Mary, walkin' arm in arm.

Here, good alive, jes let me hev a come.
Git down my bonnet off o' that ere shelf.
Well, on my life, I never did; by gum,
I reckon she's a fancyin' of harself.

Mary, here, Mary, jes you come and look.
There come owd Sally-see her dress, the skart
A-hangin' down-that fare to want a hook-
See how tha's draggin' in the dust and dart.

Good gracious, Mary, jes to look at that!
Fancy young Jim a-walking out with har!
d'yer see them feathers sticking in her 'at?
They're limsy? I should rather think they' are.

Jealous? What me? O' sech as har indeed!
Nao, that I ent, so there. Good lor',
Upon my life I think I never seed
A gal look sech a bag o' rags afore.

Me jealous? Nao, I don't care that for Jim,
I towd him I was thankful to be rid.
You never h'ard me say I cared for him,
Nao, Mary, that I knaow you never did.

I shouldn't like, not me. Hulloa, my eye,
I do believe they're comin' through the gaite.
Look Mary, ent thay tarnin' down this way?
Do, I'll stand here, an' give it to 'em straight.

Mary, look sharp an' git yer bonnet on,
An' stand 'longside o' me here while they pass.
Come, look alive now, don't they'll soon be gone;
Ah, now they've tarned the t'other side the grass.

Tha's where they're gooin', are they? Pas' the mill,
Along the fiel' path leadin' tard the woods;
I'll give he what for some day, that I will,
For walkin' out 'ith that ere bit of goods.

J'yer hear him call "Good arternune" to me?
He think he's doin' of it there some tune.
Next time I ketch him out along o' she,
Blest if I don't give he "good arternune."

"My booy Jim"
(A ballad of paternal pride)

I FEEL that wholly daized, I do 'ndeed,
That I carn scarce believe it, that's a fac';
Well, there, I knaown I never thought t'a seed
My Jim a swell like that when he come back.

He bin out forrin nigh on twenty year.
You bin out forrin, sir, when you's a lad?
You may a comed acrost my booy out theer,
But lor, you wou'nt a knaown him if yer had.

He come right up to our owd cott'ge door
Las' evenin' time. Good night! he maide us stare,
"An' how's the dad?" he say, "an' Missus? Lor,
You mighter knock me down, I do declare.

He got on one o' them there chimbley hats,
A pair of yaller gloves, a walkin' stick,
One o' them wotchercallums-them crawats-
I tell yer, he looked reg'lar up to Dick.

"Well, there," I says, "You minter say you're Jim?"
"I do, he say. Says I", "Well, tha's a bit!"
I couldn't scarce believe as that were him,
For when he left he worn't much more'n a chit.

You oughter sin th' owd woman! She was struck
All of a heap, an' cou'nt tell what to say,
He come in an' set down, she olbut shruck
Till he jes died o' larfin, pretty nigh.

My, dint he larf! He fairly shuk the stool
As we kep' gahpin at him there s' grand.
"Father," he say, "you said I were a fool
When twenty year agao I lef' the land."

Well, he kep' on a torkin' there, an' arst
All what had happened since he went away;
But there, he torkt s' precious queer, at farst
You couldn't unnerstand a wahrd he say.

But he set there as happy as yer please,
An' Missus laid the supper while he tork;
A prahper set out, too, fat pork an' peas-
"Jim olluz was a mark," she say, "on pork."

He larft, but there, the way he took that pork!
"Tha's right enough," I says, "tha's Jim, I knaow;"
But lor, he heft them peas up on his fork!
Two at a time, my stars, sir, somethin' slaow!

Well, I carn tell yer all he say las' night,
Y'll hev to hear him, sir, yerself, I doubt.
Y'll find him jest a master one to praite-
Nothin' alive that booy don't knaow about.

He bin to plaices where the sun don't set-
The tother side the warld, I think it were.
That's very like, sir, you an' him ha' met,
He sim to knaow 'most everyone out there.

He gone up to the Rect'ry, sir, to-day
To see our Parson-'ont he maike him look?
I reckon, sir, as my owd gal ud say,
Them two'll tork together like a book.

Wh', there he come, a walkin' 'ith them chaps,
There in the four-want - way, atween them carts.
Tha's my booy Jim, an' now y'll knaow, prehaps,
If you ha' sin him, sir, in forrin parts.

"Owd Bill"
(A ballad of artfulness)

OWD Bill! Why everybody knaow owd Bill;
He's olluz schemin,' olluz at some gaime,
Olluz a actin', tha's what he is; still
You can't help likin' of him all the saime.

A rum un? I sh'd rather think he were!
T'd taike yer all yer time to tackle he.
An' langwidge? Lor, j'yer ever hear him swear?
A mark on swearin'? Ah, sir, that he be.

You might as lief be talkin' to a paost
As try to maike owd Bill amen' his ways;
He knaow his way about as well as maost-
I ne'er see sich a chap in my born days.

You on'y got to say "I bet yer don't,"
An' Bill 'll do it, don' care what it be.
He'll best yer, too, I'm bothered if he 'ont ;
There's no man livin' dussent tackle he.

Las' Michaelmas us fellers got him on
Down at the Anchor, Sunday dinner time.
There was a good few on us-me, an' John,
An' Steve, an' Tom, an' Sandy Wha's-his-naime.

I don't ezackly knaow how that began.
Several come in-along the rest was Mike.
"Owd Bill," he say, "I'll lay a tanner, man,
As you carn't eat a pound o' raw bif staike."

Owd Bill, o' course, he took him like a shot,
Blest if he didn't do it, too, an' so!
A pound o' raw bif staike! He et the lot,
An' taters, an' a dish of broccolo.

He never goo to Charch, a Sunday, Bill,
Excep' he keep a larkin' all the time.
A reglar bad un, tha's what he is; still
You carn't help likin' of him all the saime.

Why, up at Mis'ley-that there poachin' fray,
I'll lay yer tuppence Bill was in the spree,
But he can olluz faike the thing some way
Afore the Magistrates, so he git free.

He done it, right enough. You woon believe
The times an' times I sin him arter hares.
I could a towd 'em thay was up his sleeve-
Nao, not the rabbits, sir, nao, nao, the snares.

Oo, he's the artfullest you ever knaowed;
He never taike no hart, not anywhere.
There's nao mistake, Bill, he's as owd as owd,
He's best the very Owd-un, I declare.

Nowhere there ent a bad un t'ekal he-
I knaow there ent a bigger liar livin',
Yet when the day of Judgmen' come you'll see,
He'll faike it somehow so he git to Hiven.

"These new-fangled ways"
(A ballad of protest)

ME, nao, sir, I don't howd 'ith these Board Schools;
Thay larn the booys too much, my thinkin, now.
An' what I see, there's jest as many fools
As when thay put the young uns to the plough.

I ent owd-fashn'd, nao, I loike to see
The young uns comin' on. But now-a-days
They say an' do sich things git over me,
An' I carnt howd 'ith these new-fangled ways.

I howd 'ith larnin, mind, but let 'em larn
Saime way as I did, not that stuff o' theirs.
Larn 'em the proper way to thetch a barn,
Larn 'em the way to sao a field o' tares.

Geoggerfy! Now what on arth's the sense
A larnin' of 'em how the moon go roun'?
An' all about Ameriky an' Frence,
An' plaices tother side o' Lunnon town?

My booy he come to me the tother night,
"D'yer knaow," he say, "the Warld an' you an' me
Are tarnin' on our axles-sich a raite
You woon believe? But there, tha's right," says he.

I tarned he on his axles, you be boun',
I cop he one. That maide me reg'lar riled,
That fairly did. The Warld a tarnin' roun'!
To hear sich stuff an' nons'nse from a child!

N' more I don't howd with them thingmibobs,
Them Parish Councils wot they started now.
There's Tom an' Harry think they're reg'lar nobs,
Cos thay goo there a kickin' up a row.

Look at that Council meetin' here las' week-
Why bless my saoul if Tom din taike the chair,
An' Parson settin' 'gin the door as meek
As some owd sheep, I tell yer; that he were.

An' what d'yer think they done? wh' nought, o' course,
Cos there aint nothin' here want doin' to.
N' wonner Parson he look drefful cross
Comin' away; I see him, didn't you?

An' I don't howd 'ith these ere ways at Charch-
A singin o' the Scripters an' that ere,
Dressin' theirselves in nightgownds stiff wi' starch:
The Boible never tell 'em that, I swear.

They say Ahmen instead o' Aimen now;
Tha's only jes to be contrairy like,
An' when that come the "Glory be" thay bow
An' cartsey, Lor, I'd like to gim a shaike.

D'yer think the Aingels sing Ahmen? Not thay,
An' when these ere are dead an' gone th'll see,
Th'll give it to 'em straight up their, th'll say
"You ent a go'n to sing along o' we."

I ent owd-fashioned, nao, I loike to see
The young uns comin' on. But now-a-days
They say an' do sich things git over me,
An' I carnt howd 'ith these new-fangled ways.

"Tell you for why"
(A ballad of logic)

Cummish'ners thay call theirsels, I'm blaowed.
A comin' roun' to see why farms don' pay!
I could a towd 'em what thay never knaowed,
Tellyerferwy-acos I could, tha's why.

One of 'em come to Master at the Hall,
An' arst all manner stuff, and writ it down.
A great owd book he'd got, to howd it all,
An' take it up to thay in Lunnon town.

Cummish'ner, I'd cummish'ner him, I would.
I could a made he look, I could to-day.
What do he knaow? He carnt do we nao good,
Tellyerferwy-acos he carnt, tha's why.

Nex' day there's Master stood we chaps a drink.
"Dessay you think that bloke a fool?" he say.
"Think ? "I says, "nao, sir, we don' want to think,
Tellyerferwy-acos we knaow, tha's why."

"Protection," Master say, "tha's what we want,
A forty-shillun duty, chaps, 'ud pay."
But he ont get it-lay yer sixpence on't.
Tellyerferwy-acos he ont, tha's why.

But what a thing that is for me an' you,
Free Traide-tha's ruination, Master say,
Tha's no good saying what they oughter do.
Tellyerferwy-'cos do they don't, tha's why.

I wish as Master were our Member; lor,
He'd larn 'em suffen, wouldn't he, my eye?
Free traiders! I guess he'd give thay what for.
Tellyerferwy-he'd Free traide them, tha's why.

He could a maide owd Harc't set up straight.
He could a twisted he about some tune,
Saime as he did them chaps what come an' praite
Up on the Green one evenin'-time las' June.

He says, says he, "You move that ere red van
Off o' my fild, don't I'll larn you who's who.
Look slippy now, and take that off my lan,'
Tellyerferwy," he say !-" 'cos don't I do."

Look at that clock! Another glass o' stout?
I thank y' sir, I doubt we dussen stay.
Do, I shoon' mind, but there, we'd best clear out,
Tellyerferwy-acos o' Bruce, tha's why.

"Never been to Colchester"
(A ballad of the Tendring Hundred)

I see young Nat come outer his,
As I come outer mine,
"An' where you off to, booy?" I sez,
"You're dressed up somethin' fine!"

"I'm gooin' by the trine," he say,
"In harf an hour or sao,
"I'm goon to Caochester to-day,"
He say, "if you must knaow."

He'd never bin to Caochester!
He hadn't I'll be boun'.
Well, that's a caution, ent it, sir,
He'd never sin the town!

He oughter went next Saddy, sir,
When I shall be a goon,
For tha's the day for Caochester-
A Saddy arternoon.

I towd 'im so; "You want to gao
A market day," sez I,
"To see the people; you don't knaow
The crowds an' crowds," I say.

"An all them little stalls an' that,
Along the High Street, lor,
I see," I sez, sez I, "young Nat,
You never bin afore.

"There's rabbuts, bards, an' guinea pigs,
An' sweets o' every kind,
An' knives and tools an' thingmijigs-
All manner o' sorts you'll find.

"An' fish an' 'ysters-don't they scent?
An' how them chaps can shout!
An' wilks all ready, so they ent
No trouble gitten out.

"An' where S'n Runnel's was, a lot
O' cheap jacks in a ring
Keep sellin' I carn tell yer wot-
Why every mortal thing.

"Yes, tha's the day to see the town
Along o' all yer pals.
An' keep a walkin' up an' down
An' talkin' to the gals."

"Well, I carn stop," he say, "good luck!"
An off goo Marster Nat.
He got a peacock's feather stuck
Jes so like in his hat.

"Well, hurry up," I sez, sez I.
An' take care o' yersel.
You got no time to lose, good-bye,
Goo'-bye, an' fare ye well.

There come the trine, you're all behin',
You'd best be starten forth,
An' you git out at Buttles, min',
Don't you'll goo roun' the North!

"The death of Mike"
(A ballad of mournfulness)

Howd me up a little, Martha, so as I can look around;
Lor, I feel that cowd an' weak, jes' wrap my showders in your gownd.
I'm a dyin', ent I, Martha? I don't scarcely recollec'
Who I be or where I bin to-I'm a dyin' I expec'.

Guess I bin a dreamin', Martha, what I min I thought jes now
I were in the Warkus, wond'rin when I got in there an' how.
Oo, that wor a laonesome feelin', wonnerful good news that seem
When I knaow tha's all onreal-that were nahthin but a dream.

Howd me up a minute, Martha, open that ere winder there.
Op' it wider, ah, tha's better, so I git a breath o' air,
So I see the fiel's an' that, an' knaow I ent a dreamin' still,
So I know that ent the Warkus, where I be a lyin' ill.

I'm a dyin', ent I, Martha? Howd my han' and don't you gao.
Don' keep on a cryin', missus, you've no call for frettin' sao.
Carn' think what'll come o' you, though, poor owd gal, when I be gone.
Don' keep on a cryin', Martha; I carn bear you talkin' on.

Martha, if I goo to-night, remember me upon yer knees.
Pray for me, an' I say, Martha, min' you think an' tell the bees.
Don't tha's sartin sure to bring some trouble to yer, I'm afraid.
Whisper to 'em softly, Martha, same as when poor Emmie died.

Lor, I do feel drefful queer, I reckon I shall goo to-night,
I can feel m'self a sinkin', I sharn see the mornin' light.
Howd me up a little, Martha, so I git a breath o' air.
Tha's more easy-like; now Martha, let me try an' say a prayer.

MIKE'S PRAYER.

"God A'mighty, I'm a dyin'; tek I pray my saoul to Hiven.
Mebbe I ha' bin a bad un, do I hop' to be forgiven.
Lord, I knaow I bin a bad un, an' I knaow I dussent baost
But I ent bin 'n the public for a twelve-m'nth as Thou knaowst.

"God A'mighty, tell my darter Emmie up in heaven with Thee,
I'm a comin' up 'longside her, evermore to live with she,
Tell her, Lord, I bin as saober these twelve months as any liven';
Don't she on' believe her father ever could a bin forgiven.

"Lord, I pray look arter Martha, till from this ere warld she gao,
Don' I carn see who's to help her, poor owd gal, when I'm laid laow,
'Less it be the rev'rent Johnson; Lord, Thou knaowest him, I guess -
Him what maide me leave the drinkin', an' give Martha that owd dress.

"Lord, I dew believe in him who died upon the cross for we,
Which I thank'm, God A'mighty; tell him sao, I pray from me,
I carn say n' more, I fare to feel as pow'rless as a mouse,
But look arter poor owd Martha, don't she'll goo 'ithin the House.'

"Another psalm of life"
(What the editor said to the palmist)

ASK me not, in mournful queries,
Why the verses that you send
Month by month, in constant series,
Are declined with thanks, my friend.

"Want of space-"you don't believe it?
Well, we own that was a lie.
Please in confidence receive it,
And we'll tell you really why.

Faultless are your lines in rhythm,
All your rhymes are quite complete,
Nothing is the matter with them,
Every verse is honey-sweet.

In the poet's proud profession
What you lack is-can't you guess?
You're a genius at expression,
But - you've nothing to express.

Poems by Charles Benham

The legend of St John's Abbey, Colchester

When William the Second was King of this land
The people of Colchester cleverly planned
A request that a man who was William's right hand,
Named Eudo, a Norman, as I understand,
Should at once be sent down to govern the town,
Because they knew well that that man of renown,
Who was truer than steel, could do a good deal
To deliver the town from stern tyranny's heel.
For in Colchester, certainly, things had been rather
Too hot in the days of King Rufus's father.

Their humble petition they made with submission,
And the King granted all without any condition.
So Eudo came down, and was hailed in the town
With hip, hip, hurrahs from papas and mammas,
And the little ones' shouting the police could not drown.
Things went very well, so the chroniclers tell,
And the town was quite happy, for Eudo the Dapifer-
Such was his title-relieved the distressed
And eased all the oppressed,

And removed from folk's backs full many a tax.
He built, too, the Castle, and Moot Hall, and opposite,
Found for his own house, as he thought, a proper site,
And then he resolved how he best could provide
For the wealth of the soul which he carried inside.
To the south of the town lived a man in a gown
Named Siric, a priest of unwonted renown,
For near his house stood a Church built of wood,
A wonderful place for miraculous grace.
And there in dark nights were seen heavenly lights,

And though some said "Absurd" others vowed they had heard
Strange voices when no one there uttered a word.
And here in this Church of St. John, on a day
It happened a certain poor man went to pray,
A man who was forced, by the King's own command,
To wear iron shackles on foot and on hand,
And there, on the feast of St. John, with a clang
His fetters went flying and made such a bang
That it quite put a stop to the hymn the choir sang,
And the whole of the town with the miracle rang.

Be all this as it might, Eudo thought that no site
In the whole of the town was so suitable quite
For a monastery's walls, and no saint could be bettered

As patron, than he who this man had unfettered.
So he worked with a will, and by next year the whole
Of the work was achieved for the good of his soul.
Two monks he placed there, the stipend to share,
To watch and to pray by night and by day,

And masses to say in the regular way,
And a smile of beautified radiance stole
O'er his face, and his eyes gave a heavenly roll
As he piously sighed, "Well, at least I have tried My best to provide
From my bodily wealth for the wealth of my soul."
But, alas, those two monks turned out terrible skunks,
And grumbled and swore they were scantily fed;
They complained that the cheese was too hard, and the bread
was too stale, and the butter was rancid, they said,
and one of them wanted a nice feather bed.
But Eudo gave both monks a "sacking" instead,
And appointed two more, who were worse than before,
For they worried poor Eudo by day and by night,
And struck, as we say, for an increase of pay,
Till he wished that he never had made the endeavour
To work for the good of his soul in this way.
At last he gave over the whole of his care
To Stephen, the Abbot of York, with a prayer
That he kindly would manage the wretched affair,
And quickly the Abbot made everything square.
Twelve monks he installed and another one called,

"By permission," a prior, a title much higher,
In fact, it's a sort of monastic esquire.
In time they elected one monk as their Abbot,
Choosing one who was quite the least likely to grab at
The wealth of the place-not a man of capacity,
But-to quote from Morant-"of no worldly sagacity."
Yet, alas for poor Eudo, the good of his soul
Still appeared to be just as far off as the Pole,
For all sorts of disputes with the Abbot arose,
And at last he resigned, and then nobody knows
What fresh troubles arose, which certainly shows
That the soul of poor Eudo could find no repose.

The good man at last to the spirit-world passed,
And there let us hope he attained to a goal
Where at length he discovered true wealth for his soul,
And his dying request was that all he loved best
Should be by the monks of the Abbey possessed.
He bequeathed them his ring with a topaz enshrined,
And a gold covered-cup to be used when they dined,
And presents of money and presents of kind,
And his mule and his horse to their care he consigned,
Then calmly to Heaven his spirit resigned.
And he begged they would pray both night and by day,
And masses would say, in the regular way,
For what he in vain had been seeking the whole
Of his life-the repose and the good of his soul.

Let all who aspire to a noble desire
For the good of their souls, recollect they require
No mortar and bricks for their sin,
Nor by building outside can they ever provide
For the soul that is builded within.

The legend of the Essex Serpent

In the year 1669 there was published in London, by Peter Lillicrap, a strange pamphlet entitled "The Flying Serpent, or Strange News out of Essex, being a true relation of a monstrous Serpent, which hath divers (diverse) times been seen at a parish called Henham-on-the-Mount, within four miles of Saffron Walden; showing the length, proportion, and bigness of the Serpent, the place where it commonly lurks, and what means have been used to kill it."

It is Christmas night, and the yule log bright
Sinks on the hearth in its own red light,
The candles burn in their sockets low;
The children must now to their slumbers go,
To dream of holly and mistletoe.
"But stay, oh stay," the children say,
"We cannot yet be sent away.
Till grandpapa there in his old arm chair
Tells us a story, we all declare
We'll none of us set a foot on the stair."
"Ah well, ah well, a tale I'll tell,
So sit down and listen, Tom, Harry and Nell,
And Sarah, and Bobby, and Johnny as well;
You must all come near, and you all shall hear
The tale that I tell to you every year."
Then the children gathered and shrieked with glee,
And the youngest sat on her grandpa's knee.
"Yes, tell us that story, please, grandpa, dear,
The story you tell us every year."
"Well, well, my children, 'twas long ago,
When I was no bigger than Tom, you know,
That my grandfather sat in his old arm chair,
With me at his feet, as it might be there,
And the tale that he told me, I tell to you,
A tale that is wonderful, strange and true."
"Hurrah, hurrah, for Grandpapa!"
And then in a trice as still as mice
To hear the old story for ever new-
"The tale which your grandpapa told to you,
The tale that is wonderful, strange and true."
"Oh, well, my dears, it's a hundred years
Since my grandfather came from the Northern shires
To settle in Essex by Henham Hill,
In the house where your cousins are living still,
Though the village is not what it used to be
When I went to stay there in '43.

These Essex Ballad's were written between 1892 and 1895 by Charles Edwin Benham. They are among the finest dialect poems in English, capturing not only the words and phrases of the Essex rural labourer, but his wit and wisdom too.

If you have enjoyed reading the ballads and poems contained within this book, why not listen to a recording made simulating the actual dialect of that period. The ballads are spoken in the Essex dialect by four talented local people, Geoff Bowery; Jane Dansie; Westley Sandford and Alan Snelling, between them, they have successfully reproduced the fast disappearing North Essex accent, this recording from the "Colchester Recalled Oral History Group" is available c/o Andrew Phillips, 19 Victoria Road Colchester, Essex, and is highly recommended as an aid to this book.
Also included in this recording is a rare recording of Charles Edwin Benham himself.

The commentary was written by Colchester's historian, Andrew Phillips, and is spoken by Sheila Foster and Peter Kerr.

Poems by Nicholas Olde & Ken Sharpe

The following poems were written by Mr. Amian Lister Champneys who wrote under the pen-name of "Nicholas Olde". Mr. Champneys who was born in 1880, referred to himself as 'Old Nick', he was a local man who moved into Thorrington in 1936, staying until his death in 1951.

Among the many poems that he wrote was, "An English Churchyard", referring of course to his local Church in Thorrington, the Rev. Grant, who was a minister of St. Mary Magdalen Church at the time had this particular poem hung in his church where it still hangs to this day.

Mr. Champneys wrote two books of poems, namely, "The Pageant of Progress", and "The Last Goddess".

I have selected a few poems from each of these books that I thought the reader might enjoy, they depict life as it was in the surrounding area of Thorrington and the Tendring Hundred District in the early part of this century.

Another Thorrington poet is Ken Sharpe, who, in a very short space of time has established himself as a skilled and competent writer of poems and has written under very difficult circumstances.

Following the successful removal of cataracts in both eyes in 1991, Ken very quickly discovered that Glaucoma had set in rendering him totally blind.

His writing of poetry came about as a direct result of his blindness, and has filled a very large gap in his life that might otherwise have been lacking. I hope this explanation and his poems will inspire others in similar situations not to give up in such difficult circumstances.

Finally, this last section also includes some poems that I have chosen at random from the early and latter part of this century.

Blindness

When the shutters came down over my eyes,
Very black and grey became all my skies,
So I determined to sit in a chair,
And do nothing all day-but just stare.

But when in the garden I sat down,
Then very soon a smile replaced my frown,
For I quickly found that seeing didn't matter,
So long as I heard bird's quiet chatter.

For in God's world I now truly know
That a badly dented faith can still regrow.
His quiet word comes just like a balm
And his promise is like a wondrous charm.

So when your world is grey and black,
And you can't look forward or even back,
Remember these words so simple yet true,
As Christ said-
I am always with you.

Ken Sharpe

The Broken Barge

On Brightlingsea's muddy banks lies the dark bulk
Of an old wooden sailing barge's abandoned hulk,
Its wooden decking is all stripped bare,
While hull gapes open to onlookers stare.
No longer will waves part from its bow
So slimy green sea moss garlands its prow.
The solitary crew is now a white gull
Hunting crabs or fish hiding in the hull.
For many years now the indifferent North Sea
Has through the barge flowed grey and free.
Each summer past the barge's crumbling timbers grim,
Sail modern plastic pleasure craft, jaunty and trim.
Forgotten are the barge's halcyon days of sail
When wind pressure made her dip its' rail.
Long gone are her leeboards, ropes and gear,
Used when she traded coastwise far and near.
With sixty ton of cargo in her hold,
Navigating East Anglia's coastline in days of old.
Laden with corn from Beaumont-Cum-Moze quay
Then sailing the dangerous trackless expanse of sea.
Then threading up through the bustling Thames river
And finding where her grain had to deliver.
With ballast of London clay within the week
She'd grounded at the head of Alresford Creek.
Her hull was made like a date-box outside
So she could sail a river at low tide.
Sticky clay was replaced by a potatoe crop,
At Ipswich, her next port to stop.
Her many dull humdrum trading years were spent
Carrying Britain's goods as she came and went.
But after the Second World War trade accelerated
And the worn out old barge became outdated.
Used for towing, she gave up the ghost
And is finishing her days on Brightlingsea.s coast.

Ken Sharpe.

Old Barge remains on the Causeway, Brightlingsea

Ghost Railway

No longer do trains frighten seagull and rook,
While passengers crane heads out for a look.
A long time ago, in days gone past,
Trains connected Brightlingsea with Colchester, sleek and fast.
But the branch line has since closed down
And trains no longer travel from Brightlingsea town.
Over Brightlingsea station the Community Centre now stands.
While fluffy rabbits scamper over British Rail lands.
Bushes and wild shrubs on railway embankment encroach
Where once clanked the dusty coupled passenger coach.
The cinder track bed is now the haunt
Of the bumble-bee, butterfly and bramble gaunt.
Walkers, picnickers and lovers stroll the permanant way,
While autumnal blackberry hunters scan each bramble spray.
Silent cold grey depths of the River Colne
Glide beside the track with scarcely a moan.
Weeds, grass and bushes invade more every year.
Giving wild creatures cover, their young to rear.
Nature crept back and lovingly reclaimed her own,
Forgotten now is the Diesel Locomotive's mournful moan.
Mother Nature flung down her concealing verdant gown,
Covering old railway scars that made God frown!

Ken Sharpe

Photograph of Brightlingsea's Railway Station in the 1930's

Spring

Laughing April

The fresh-faced Housemaid of the sky,
With all her petticoats pinned high,
Has set each table, stool and chair,
And all the furniture up there,
Apile beneath the snow-white shrouds
That you and I, dear, call the clouds.

And now, before she scrubs the floors,
She sends the young Winds out of doors,
And bids them take themselves away
And go down on the Earth to play;
And here they come, the romping flirts,
To tumble Dolly's hair and skirts.

The Angelic Housemaid takes no care,
But sosses water everywhere
Over the shining heavenly floors
Till down upon the Earth it pours;
And only laughs to see she's wet
An earthly lover and his pet.

London

I often go to Colchester,
Now Peggy's in the shop;
But, though I'm close on sixty years,
I've never been up top.

Last week I talked o' goin'
Along o' Joseph Wood
To Smithfield, but the missis say
She didn't want I should.

And just as well I didn't too!
Do, I'd ha' lost my way,
The same as Joe, perhaps, and not
Got home 'fore Saturday.

He got to London right enough,
And went in to the show:
Then sudden-like, saw by the clock
That that were time to go.

Well, up in London, Joseph say,
(Leastways so they told he),
They've half-a-dozen stations-quite;
Which don't fare right to me.

And so, when Joseph tried to find
The one by which he came,
Why, no one couldn't tell him,
For he didn't know its name.

And Joseph, who was never one
To set much store by talk,
Thinks, Well if I can't get the train,
I be a-goin' to walk.

So he say to a policeman
At the corner o' the square,
Which way to Al'sford Pointer?
I can find my way from there.

Well, p'raps you won't believe me,
But the fellow didn't know;
And, when Joe told him what he thought,
He went on ever so.

And in the end he run him in;
And how Joe must ha' swore
When his return-half ticket
Fell out upon the floor!

So they sent him home on Saturday,
And made him pay excess;
And the station-master tell him
As he ain't got no redress.

No! I don't hold with London,
Though they've colleges and schools.
Never heard of Al'sford Pointer!
Why! I reckon they be fools.

The Pointer

The voice of the village

The doubtful Bachelor

'Most every man that's married
Would be better off alone:
Still, I don't mind a wedding,
So be that ain't my own.
I was best man up at Weeley,
When Lucy married Jim;
But, though I like the pair of them,
I didn't envy him;
For I shouldn't care for marriage-
Though I fared to think I should,
When I went picking bluebells
With the bride's-maid in the wood.

I wholly like a pretty girl
To cuddle and to kiss;
But, as for getting married-
Well, what I think is this:
I'd have a lot of howling babes
A-sprawling round the house;
And, when they're sleeping, have to keep
As quiet as a mouse.
I couldn't go on same as that-
And yet I've thought I could,
Since I went picking bluebells
With the bride's-maid in the wood.

The Rangers Daughter

O, I am in love with the ranger's daughter,
And she is in love with me;
And here are the sweeties that I have brought her,
But none is so sweet as she.

The ranger's daughter has eyes that dart
Swift glances of frolic and fun
With as sure an aim at her victim's heart
As ever her father's gun.

And the ranger's daughter has long, black hair,
All braided in artful coils;
And my heart is the captive that's caught in their snare,
Like the prey of her father's toils.

But I have the heart of the ranger's daughter,
So she shall keep mine for me;
And here are the sweeties that I have brought her,
Though none is so sweet as she.

Dolly's Fairing

When Joe took Dolly in to town
To see the Fat-stock Show,
He said he'd buy the girl a gown:
A right good gown, says Joe;
For I wholly like that girl, says he,
And I don't care what I spend on she.

So Dolly she were something glad.
Says, she, I'll have a pink.
I'm pleased to think I've such a lad.
I'm lucky, don't you think,
To get one that's so kind as he?
For he don't care what he spend on me.

Well, after they had seen the stock
And crowds of men and women,
Now, girl, Joe say, we'll buy that frock;
But first we'll get the trimmin';
For I wholly like you: that I do!
And I don't care what I spend on you.

They found a shop and Joe he say,
Some ribbons, if you please.
The man he fetches down a tray:
Says Joe, Ay, some like these;
For I wholly like the girl, says he,
And I don't care what I spend on she.

Says Dolly, There now Joe! I think
I'll have this, if I can.
How much, says Joe, for this here pink?
Why, twopence, says the man.
Then I'll have half a yard, Joe say,
For I don't care what I spend to-day.

Now shall we get the frock? Doll say.
Says Joe, That's goin' to rain.
Pity to spoil it straightaway:
So shall we come again
Next year? Then p'r'aps I'll buy you two,
For I don't care what I spend on you.

The Penalty of Health

That's like a hospital at ours:
There's Father run a bush
Into his thumb: right swoll' that be;
And Mother, she've a push
Just where her corset presses her;
And May, she don't fare right:-
A gastric stomach, doctor say,
When he come round last night.
Take egg and milk, he say to she;
But she can't come an egg:-
Then there be Albert got a gre't
Old gumboil on his leg;
And George, he cut his thumb right deep,
Buck-heading of a hedge,
Along o' using Albert's rip
What hasn't got no edge.
And Dolly went last night to see
The circus what's in town,
And now she've got the belly-ache
From laughing at the clown.
Then, Arthur, he's fell off his load
And got to lay and rest;
And Fred can't go to work because
The dew get on his chest.
So fares we've all got something wrong-
Except o' course poor me.
As has to slave from dawn to dark
To do the work o' three.

"We was lucky mother"
"Finding us a bed like this"

Summer

The Brook

Come down, love, into the meadow
Where the yellow king-cup grows
And the brooklet whispers secrets
To the rushes as he flows.
Let his waters clear and sweet
Eddy round your little feet.

But do not too rashly venture,
Though he now flows cool and chaste,
Lest, by that warm contact maddened,
He engulf you to your waist;
For your charms might surely fire
Even water with desire.

Yet the brook's a fickle lover,
Whose last mistress is the sea.
Let him seek her cold embrace:
You shall have more joy of me,
That am flesh and blood like you,
With a heart that's warm and true.

Horses

My Nelly don't like ho'ses:
They're such gre't old things, she say;
And if she see one in a field
She go another way:
She go another way to work,
Do my Nelly if she can;
But she ain't afreard o' ho'ses
When she be with a man.

Huge, high ho'ses
A-pawin' up the ground!
Gre't old ho'ses!
Nelly must go round.
Nelly is so gentle,
And Nelly is so small,
And they gre't old ho'ses
Be so terrible and tall.

No, Nelly don't like ho'ses:
They're such fierce old things, she say;
And, if she see one coming,
She'll scream and run away.
She'll go through mud and water
To avoid 'em if she can;
But she ain't afeard o' nothing
When she be with a man.

Huge hugh ho'ses
A-tearin' up the grass!
Fierce old ho'ses!
Won't let Nelly pass.
Nelly is so gentle,
And Nelly is so small;
And they gre't old ho'ses
Be so terrible and tall.

The Stupid Man

I met a man along the road
I'd never seen before.
Good evening, miss, he said, and then
Was going to say more;
But I saw what he wanted,
And so I turned and ran;
But he caught me up and kissed me.
O, he was a stupid man!

And he put his arm around my waist
And took me down the lane,
And set me down upon the grass,
Though that was wet with rain
And wetted all my petticoats;
And then, when I began
To cry, said he was sorry.
O, he was a stupid man!

And when at last we came away,
(And, O dear! that was late),
He hugged me tight and kissed me
As we stood against the gate,
Saying, Sweetheart, will you meet me
To-morrow, if you can?
But maybe you don't want to.
O, he was a stupid man.

Katy

My Katy's gone to Colchester:
I hope she won't be long:
There's some o' them there soldier chaps
As don't know right from wrong.
She has such merry, laughing eyes,
Such dainty little curls;
And the soldier-boys they will be boys,
And the girls they will be girls.

I wish that she were back again:
I hope she won't be late:
The time that always go so slow
When one has got to wait.
She has such pretty, pouted lips:
Such dimples in her cheek;
And when I've waited half an hour
That fare more like a week.

That won't be long before that's dark:
I hope she'll be back soon:
I don't want she should pass the wood
With no light but the moon.
She looks so sweet by daylight
As nothing could be sweeter;
But when the moon shines on her-! Yes,
I think I'll go and meet her.

The Descent of Man

The young man's eyes are keen and clear:
He should see more than we;
But the pride of youth blindfolds him,
And so he cannot see,
In his folly, that his father is a better man than he.

But you and I are middle-aged
And have a wider view;
And our eyes have learned to filter
False semblances from true;
And so I'm sure your father was a better man than you.

And perhaps, as I grow older
And wiser, by and by,
I may see yet more clearly
And admit, before I die,
That possibly my father was a better man than I.

Indeed there's not a man alive,
And hardly any dead
Or yet to be, of whom the same
May not be justly said.
So perhaps, in spite of Progress-
If such a thing there be-
The Apes that are our ancestors were better men than we.

The Road Hog

The consequential motorist
(O execrable word!)
Sits at his little wheel and looks
As blissfully absurd
As some best-selling novelist
Posed for his tame photographist.

The fat, contemptuous motorist
Thinks walking infra dig.,
But knows not that his vacuous face
Is very like a pig:-
A globose Old Spot medallist
Scorning some lean abstentionist.

The supercilious motorist,
Who sneers at men with legs,
Will crack his bald skull one fine day,
As sure as eggs is eggs;
And men with legs will then assist
In burying the motorist.

Wisdom and Knowledge

The Man of Science rather thinks
The Universe is his;
And while he's very young indeed
He's pretty sure it is.

But as he grows maturer
And begins to find things out
He admits a certain access
Of philosophic doubt.

Then, if he's apt at learning,
He will go on learning till
He's learnt that what he really knows
Is practically nil.

And so in time, if he is wise,
His false claims he retracts,
And owns that Truth is everything,
While Facts are merely facts.

And, in the end perhaps he'll share
With his familier friends
The discovery that Wisdom
Begins where knowledge ends.

Autumn

One Day

I wonder, I wonder, will Dolly remember
When midsummer happened to come in November?
'Twas strange as if Brickleesey Belfry had stood
Straight up in the middle of Pudd'n'y Wood,

We all of us know that a planet will stray;
And the Earth must have strayed into Heaven that day:
So I think I'll give Dolly a little gold ring
To remind her of such a remarkable thing.

An English Churchyard

Sheltered from storm by ashes tall,
Betwixt the Hall Wood and the Hall,
Whose well-filled stackyard gleams with gold,
The little church, 'mid gravestones old,
Sleeps ever and as still.
Hence may a man gaze peacefully
Across the vale t'wards Bricklesey,
Whose church stands on a hill
Looking o'er marshes widely spread,
O'er saltings, seas and weald.
Hence may he see the flaming sun
Die glorious when his day is done,
Sure that to-morrow he shall rise
Bathed in the hues of Paradise.

* * * * *

'Mid English men and women I
Ask but to live and love and die
And 'neath the green earth with them lie
Amid these English fields.

Winter

Jack Frost

How bleak and comfortless the light
That waits on this new day!
The morning's colder than the night;
For Winter's on his way.

And on the grey panes everywhere,
While still the sky was dark,
Jack Frost, that bitter forerunner,
Has left his finger-mark.

And through the garden he has stalked,
Turning the green leaves black;
And worms lie still where he has walked,
Each frozen in its track.

So, Dolly, pull your eider quilt
Up higher to our chins,
Lest you, and I, too, haply wilt
Ere we've confessed our sins.

Colchester Garrison Rhymes

Changes

It's nothing like it used to be;
The wooden huts aren't there;
And not a soul remembered me,
As I stood near the square.

I missed the uniforms of red
That I knew years ago;
They wear the khaki now instead,
And keep the red for show.

The drill book I knew "inside out"
Is different today;
And Sergeant-Majors need not shout
When wanting their own way.

The troops they have their "schooling" now;
An education scheme;
And "Why" is taught as well as "How,"
And things are what they seem.

Such changes in the Sergeants' Mess!
And changes in the bar!
The Tommy has his "civvy" dress;
The Corporal owns a car.

It's nothing like it used to be;
The wooden huts aren't there;
And not a soul remembered me,
As I stood near the square

Betty Brown

For a fortnight come next Tuesday
I've been courting Betty Brown
In the kitchen of a morning
Before her master's down.
So on Saturday I asked her
Would she walk out one day soon;
And she said she'd go out with me
On Sunday afternoon.

So I puts on my new blue suit
And my new yellow tie;
And mother say a girl would be
Proud of a chap like I.

But when I see Bet in the street
All dolled up in her best-
Why, I never see no lady
So beautifully dressed.

I could see she still was Betty,
Though she fared so grand a person
And, tho' I'd have liked to kiss her,-
Well ! speak to her I dursn'.

No! I'll go round in the morning
Before her master's down;
For I ain't afraid o' Betty
In her plain cotton gown.

My Window Picture

I love a window, anywhere, One always sees a picure there,
All kinds of pictures, dull or fair, Pictures ev'ryone may share,
My window pictures never bore, They're ever changing, by the score;
When one has gone, there still are more, And some I simply just adore!
Within my window picture-frame, No picture's ever quite the same-Not e'en
that grand and portly dame. Sometimes "rheumatics" make her lame!
Miss Next-Door-House, her work all done, Comes out, dressed up,
to have some fun with young Tom Brown-she'll smile and run.
For her Romance has just begun! Mrs Newly-Wed, at six o'clock,
When City workers homeward flock, At garden gate, in pretty frock,
Her husband kisses! Loads in stock!
But, best of all I love to see the children playing games with glee,
And prams with chubby babies, wee, Who smile and wave their hands at me.
When buses, vans and motor-cars A noisy one there is that jars!
Have gone, my window shows me stars: Orion, Vulcan, Venus, Mars.
And so my window oft I woo, Like Cinderella's magic shoe,
To pleasant joys it is the clue-Now, don't you love a window, too?

The Little Gardener

I often help my Daddy
Hoe the garden when that's fine.
Mine's quite a little hoe, and Dad's
Is bigger far than mine;
And so is Bill's; but then, you see,
Bill's pretty nigh thirteen:-
Still Mother often say to me,
One can see where you've been.

I'll help my Dad next Easter
When he goes tater-settin',
Though mine's a little doddy spade
And my Dad's be a gre't 'un:-
Near twice as big as Bill's that be,
Though Bill's nigh on thirteen:-
Still, when Mam brings my bait to me,
She shall see where I've been.

In Memorium
"Old Forge Barkingside"

Seventeen 0 Seven till 1961
A fairish innings when all's said and done,
But now it is condemed to die,
Scotland Yard know the reason why,
"It's crime" it stands in progress way,
Obsolete like the horse drawn shay,
Once births and deaths registered here
Now no one's left to shed a tear,
Upon this site there will arise
A Police Station of wonderous size
Full of policemen bold and meek,
All earning twenty quid a week,
And some place somewhere in the sky
Where horses go to when they die
They'll neigh, look down and with a nod,
Say the place is gone where we were shod
The smithy there was a funny cuss
but always kindly treated us
We fear his future's far from good
They've pinched his bloody livelihood,
The fire is out, hearth open wide,
Hammer and Tongs are laid aside,
The anvils ring and bellows cease,
Old Forge forever rest in peace.

Although this picture does not depict the original forge at Barkingside, it is none the less typical of a blacksmith's forge of this period.

Bed-Time

Here comes a candle to light you to
bed,
So say goodnight quickly, small
Sleepy-head;
The Dustman and Dream-Man are waiting
for you,
And if they're kept waiting you know what
they'll do!
The Dream-Man won't give you a single
nice dream...
The Dustman will blow out the friendly
moonbeam.
So here is your candle, and hurry to bed,
Shut your eyes tightly and lay down your
head,
Morning comes quickly with sunshine and
song,
Hurry to sleep-it will soon be along!
Climb into bed now and blow out the light,
The Man in the Moon wants to wish you
goodnight.
When she's tucked up away we will creep,
For we mustn't wake her-she's nearly asleep.